Wild Perseverance

The History of Perseverance Wild Blueberry Farm

Lou Sidell

First edition, January 2026

ISBN 979-8-9934818-2-1 (paperback)
ISBN 979-8-9934818-3-8 (ebook)

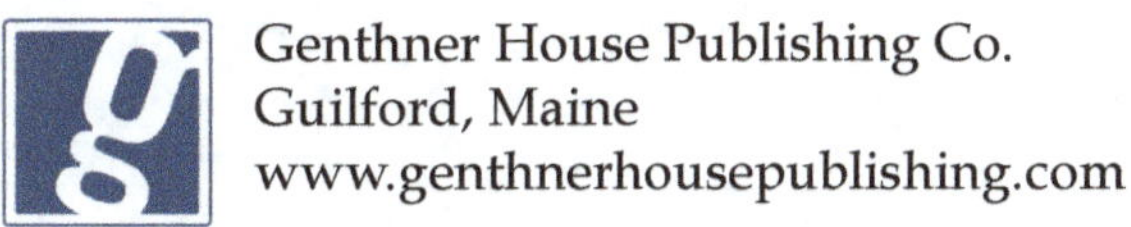 Genthner House Publishing Co.
Guilford, Maine
www.genthnerhousepublishing.com

Table of Contents

Chapter 1 — Kingsbury Plantation

In the heart of central Maine, nestled in the foothills of the beautiful northern range of the Appalachians lies the community of Kingsbury Plantation with a year-round population of around 28 people. Kingsbury Plantation with its rich history and unique blend of natural beauty, can be traced back to 1786 when William Bingham won a lottery that granted him the ownership of two million acres of land. That vast expanse includes what is now known as the present-day towns of Bingham, Kingsbury, Mayfield and even extends up the majestic Mount Katahdin.

In 1825 a devastating forest fire swept through the region, clearing a lot of the land. In 1833 the Honorable Judge Sanford Kingsbury from Gardiner, Maine purchased the land that became Kingsbury from William Bingham's heirs for a modest sum of $4,000. Another huge landowner, William Hilton and his brother, made a clearing in Kingsbury the following year. In 1835 Judge Kingsbury constructed a sawmill and grist mill at the outlet of Ford Pond, which was later renamed Kingsbury Pond.

By 1836 the population of Kingsbury had grown sufficiently enough to warrant its incorporation as a town. The town's growth continued, with the population reaching 174 by 1870 and surging to 198 just a decade later. By 1882, Kingsbury had transformed into a thriving community. According to a Gazetteer of the State of Maine, the town boasted a variety of businesses, including mechanic shops, a general store, a hotel, and the mills that had been established by Judge Kingsbury. Additionally, there were two public schools, one of which is still standing along Campbell Road in the middle of our farm; it is a testament to the solid building techniques of that century. There was also a church organization called the Buzzellites (named after John Buzzell who split from the Free Baptists in 1835) near the center of the community.

Kingsbury lies just west of the town of Abbot along State Route 16, which was once known as the Trans Maine Highway. Going west on Rt. 16 the next incorporated town is Bingham which lies along the Kennebec River. The highway is a two-lane road that is fairly straight with many hills (vertical curves). It is a scenic drive particularly captivating in the fall when the trees burst into vibrant hues of reds, yellows, and oranges. It is the only paved road in Kingsbury. Kingsbury lacks an electrical grid except for a very small section of the northeast corner; therefore, residents rely on personal generators for power. Many of the estimated 100 camps surrounding Kingsbury Pond have gas lights and gas cooking burners. Some residents have gas refrigerators and most of the residents rely on wood for heat.

Kingsbury is bordered on the north by Blanchard Township (population 91); on the east by the Town of Abbot (population 650) and a small portion of the Town of Parkman (population 747); on the south by the Town of Wellington (population 229); and on the west by Mayfield Township (population 0). Kingsbury had a population of three in 1980.

I have heard tales about what kind of a place Kingsbury was during the prohibition. There were two hotels on Route 16, one has long since vanished, but the other was later known as the Worcester house. It is a two-story white structure just off the very short Hotel Drive that crosses Kingsbury Stream. It is said that significant amounts of money from Guilford and Dover-Foxcroft exchanged hands in the backroom gambling endeavors. The woods in Kingsbury were home to numerous illegal stills. Prior to the Worcester's buying the house it served as a hotel, town office, post office and gas station.

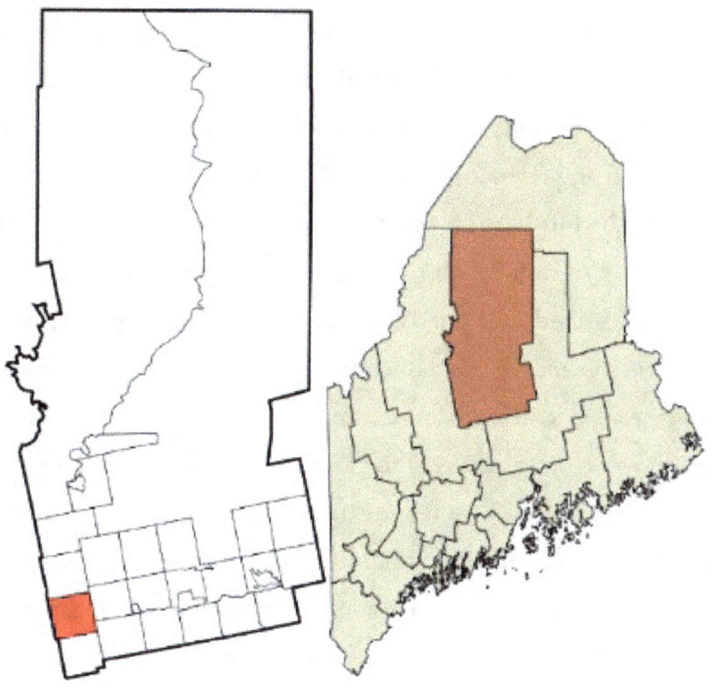

Chapter 2 — History of the Farm

Back in the late 1800's traveling east on Campbell Road as you climbed Davis Hill, the last hill before the farm, the locals referred to that area of the farm as the 'other side of Jordan.' One of the interesting facets of owning the wild blueberry farm is when the "old timers" stop by and share a little of the history of Kingsbury or stories about the farm and the Preble's. Of course, they always seem to stop by during harvest season when we are out in the fields and have no way to immediately write down all the good stuff they tell us. I have listened and tried later to write what they told me, but I know that over the years I have missed many of the intricate details.

As best we can determine, an earlier owner other than Judge Kingsbury was True Ames who purchased 50 acres prior to the Civil War for a reported $25 on what is now the north end of Perseverance Wild Blueberry Farm. In 1820 Rufus Campbell bought land in Kingsbury and according to the 1860 US Census of Agriculture he had seven improved acres and 93 unimproved acres. In 1870 Mr. Campbell had 18 acres cleared and 132 other acreage. In a discussion I had with his great-great grandson, Reverend Campbell of Sangerville, he told me that around 1835 Rufus built a Cape Cod style home that still stands on the farm today. The fields surrounding what later became the Campbell School were owned by Nathaniel Curtis. His son, George Curtis, married Mary Campbell, and they lived in a house on the far south end of the current farm. Their daughter, Ada Curtis Gourley had a son, Garnet, who managed the pick-your-own blueberry fields surrounding the schoolhouse in the

PHOTO: Barn collection of old bottles and jars from the farm.

1920's. In the early 1900's part of the southwestern corner of the farm was owned by the Snowflake Canning Company, which was owned by the Baxter Family. The family included Perciful Baxter, who became a governor of Maine and later established Baxter State Park that encompasses Mount Katahdin, Maine's highest peak. I have had older customers say they worked for Mr. Baxter during the blueberry harvest. The farm includes four lots from the original Blanchard & Kingsbury Subdivision Plan filed in the 1830s by Judge Kingsbury. It is Part of lots 1 and 2 and all of lots 3 and 4. There were five homesteads comprising the current farm.

The previous owner before our purchase, Earle Hinckley Preble, purchased his first parcel of the blueberry farm in May 1950 from Lester and Flo Ward and bought the second parcel that same year from Ada Curtis Gourley. In April 1951, he acquired the third parcel from the Snowflake Company, and he bought the fourth parcel in May 1952 from Henry Cowett. Over the next few decades, the Preble's farm became well known in southern Piscataquis County. While Mr. Preble was known for his stern way with the raking crew, he was also revered by his peers. Born in 1892, Mr. Preble was a tall man from Addison, Maine, and his early career was designing sailing ships. After his first wife died, he drove to Boston to visit his brother. In 1945 he asked his brother's neighbor, Florence Owen, out to dinner. She was a short fireplug of a woman with a great sense of humor, and early stories say she taught opera voice music. They married and he brought his bride to Addison. It was a second marriage for both. Mrs. Preble later told us her wedding day was the only time she ever saw Earl in a suit. The Preble's had a large wood frame structure on an estuary in Addison. As soon as mud season would allow, they got in Earl's Jeep and drove to Kingsbury where they usually stayed until mid-November. Mrs. Preble soon learned

PHOTO: Fairview wine bottle.

that Mr. Preble was a very frugal person. They never stopped for meals on their trips to and from the farm; they dined on kippers and crackers as the Jeep made its way to their destination. One former acquaintance of his said, "Old man Preble was so tight that he would squeeze a buffalo nickel until the buffalo shit."

Mrs. Preble took great delight in meeting people who came to pick their own berries. She loved her wine and cooking blueberry pies in the oven of the old Home Clarion wood stove, in the kitchen of the old house. The "dump" or garbage pile not far from the house at the edge of the woods is evidence of many tins of kipper containers and lots of wine bottles along with all kinds of tin cans, oil cans, and metal from household waste. I have retrieved quite a collection of old bottles that now line the walls of the barn and the mobile home. These include old ketchup and mustard bottles and jars, as well as canning jars. It is fun to explore the multiple "dump" sites on the farm.

We don't know if the Preble's had names for all the fields, but we do know that they had names for at least two of them. The field that cuts into the woods to the west of the house is known as "the bear's corner." We were told they took seven bears out of the bear's corner the year before we bought the farm. The field that lies east of the house and in front of the old Cowett homestead is known as "the sheep's pasture," according to Mrs. Preble.

Perseverance Wild Blueberry Farm is an independent farm not directly affiliated with a freezer plant and has more acreage than most independent blueberry farms in Maine. While blueberry farms owned by freezer plants typically span several thousand acres, the majority of independent growers are relatively small, ranging from a few acres to several hundred acres. At one point, Perseverance Wild Blueberry Farm was in the upper ten percentile, by acreage, among independent blueberry growers. Another distinguishing feature of Perseverance Wild Blueberry Farm is its location. Unlike most blueberry growers concentrated along the Maine Coast, particularly in Washington and Hancock Counties, Perseverance Wild Blueberry

Farm is situated in a relatively remote region. In 1992, it was among only seven commercial blueberry growers in Piscataquis County, including four in Kingsbury Plantation. We define a commercial blueberry farm as one that sells to wholesalers or freezer plants. Today, the only commercial blueberry grower in Kingsbury Plantation is the ninety acre former Worcester farm on the north side of Route 16. Perseverance Wild Blueberry Farm ceased sending blueberries to freezer plants in 2015 due to a significant drop in the price per pound that the plants were willing to pay. The price was lower than the cost of producing the harvest, let alone the cost of transporting the blueberries to the freezer plant. Although, we got two cents per pound from the freezer plant for transporting the berries. That meant that a nine hundred pound load would only yield $18 for gas money. My one-ton truck only got 10 miles per gallon, and it was 93 miles one way to the freezer plant. Sure, the two cents helped to offset the cost of gas, but the cost of operating a truck goes way beyond the cost of gas alone. At one time there were small blueberry cooperatives and freezer plants around Maine. Some consolidated while others were acquired by larger operations usually based in the coastal areas of Maine. Over time, the small growers gradually sold their operations to larger blueberry growers or to non-growers, and eventually the larger growers faced the challenge of making a profit, so they ultimately sold the land to non-growers. In some instances, freezer plant owners acquired smaller farms and consolidated their holdings, leading to a decline in the number of blueberry farms in Maine. An additional problem for Maine blueberry growers was the fact that Canadian blueberry farms are subsidized by their government. This makes Maine's market more challenging to show a profit. At the same time; however, the industry has seen an increase in the number of small organic farms operated by a younger generation. My conclusions above are not based on a scientific study but purely based on conversations with others in the industry. What sets Perseverance Wild Blueberry Farm apart from other low-bush blueberry farms is that most of its blueberry plants are 'sour tops,' (or velvet leaf) a unique species distinct from the 'low sweets' commonly found in other low-bush blueberry farms. The low sweet wild blueberry plants put most of their energy into producing fruit. The primary disadvantage of the sour top blueberry is that they are harder to rake because there are more leaves and stems. Regardless, many people believe that the sour top blueberries have a superior flavor, and I couldn't agree more.

Chapter 3 — The Sidell Story

Earl Preble died in 1985 at the age of 94, and because of his death, Mrs. Preble decided to sell the farm. Nancy's parents, Lester and Nellie Buck, were friends of the Preble's, and Mrs. Preble (now deceased) was interested in selling to the Buck's. My wife, Nancy, learned about the farm via her mother and quickly stated her strong desire to buy the farm.

I need to back up and explain how I got into this part of my life. I met Nancy at the Association of State Floodplain Managers (ASFPM) conference in New Orleans in 1985. We both lived in Illinois and we both won national recognition for developing a hazard mitigation plan for our respective communities. Both plans addressed significant mitigation for flooding. Nancy lived and worked in Kampsville, Illinois, the home of the Center for American Archeology where she was an archeological botanist, and she lived in the floodplain. I lived in West Peoria and was the planning and zoning administrator for Peoria County which had significant flooding issues. Kampsville won recognition as a small community while Peoria County was recognized as a large community. I met Nancy again a year later in Pittsburg for the ASFPM annual conference. To keep this short, let's just say one thing led to another and before I knew it, she moved in with me. I knew she was a native Mainer and that her parents, her sister and her brother-in-law owned blueberry farms in central Maine. After a few weeks of living together, Nancy announced she knew where there was a blueberry farm for sale in Maine. Nancy called Mrs. Preble and after her conversation she got off the phone full of enthusiasm saying, "It's a beautiful farm with 310 acres, and it is near a pond and has great views. It has 110 acres of blueberries, and the rest is wooded. I think we need to go look at it!"

As a Midwesterner, when someone says pond, I think of a koi pond or a farm pond for irrigation. In Maine I now know a pond is a lake. As for blueberries, I did not have a clue how they grew. They could have been on bushes, small trees, vines or who knows what. A few weeks later, Nancy had another conversation with Mrs. Preble. She was more excited about the farm than before. She hung up and started describing the farm in detail. "It is two and a half miles from Kingsbury Pond. It has an old house with gravity flow water. Kingsbury is under LURC's jurisdiction. It is off the grid and is just beautiful!"

"What do you mean, gravity-flow water?" I asked.

"There is a dug well up the hill from the old house and they ran a heavy hose underground downhill from the well to the house. Gravity makes it flow downhill to the house. They prime the well in the spring and drain it in the winter to prevent it from freezing. They didn't stay there during the winter months." replied Nancy.

"Oh, and the farm is under LURC's jurisdiction. LURC? What's that all about?" I asked.

"There is no local government, but the state manages the undeveloped areas of the state with a state agency called the Land Use Regulation Commission (LURC). It has the land use and zoning authority, and the taxes are low," Nancy continued.

My thought was when you put LURC and government in the same sentence something is not right?!

"It is off the grid, meaning there is no electricity!? I am a city boy, NO WAY! I am not living off the grid!" I proclaimed.

"Well, I already bought the airplane tickets, and they are non-refundable and, besides, you have not met mother and dad," she finished.

Near the end of April 1987, we flew into Boston and rented a car. We drove north on Interstate 95, then crossed over to Route 1 in Kittery and followed the coast up to Ellsworth, then west to Bangor, and finally Route 15 to Sebec. Nancy's parents were wonderful and welcomed me to Maine with open arms. The next morning Nancy's sister and brother-in-law, Rainy and Jim, joined us. Nancy and I piled into the Buck's Toyota van and headed west to Kingsbury. Rainy and Jim drove separately. As we drove through Guilford, I saw thousands of white birch logs scattered over the landscape. It was just one month earlier that Maine had experienced a horrible flood, and the Pride mill in Guilford had all those logs waiting to be made into golf tees. I asked Let (Lester) to stop so I could take pictures. After all, I am a floodplain manager. These pictures would make a great graphic of the power of water. Nancy told me that while I was out of the van taking pictures, Let said, "Oh, one of those!"

When we arrived at the farm we walked up to the farmhouse and after a brief introduction with Mrs. Preble, we decided to walk the farm. We began walking north through the blueberry fields. Nancy's description of the farm was accurate; it was a beautiful place. Hills and low mountains surrounded the farm, and the views were definitely picturesque. It was on the northwest field on the north slope that I had a weak moment. I turned to Nancy and said 'yes.' I soon understood that purchasing the farm was going to be a big life-altering experience. The family felt the purchase was more than Nancy and I could manage and made it clear that we should buy the farm as a joint venture. I didn't like that idea, but as the new kid to the group I kept my mouth shut and let Nancy make the decision. When we returned to the old farmhouse, Mrs. Preble was waiting for us in the kitchen. We were asked to introduce ourselves and I was the last one to speak. Mrs. Preble stopped me and said, "You talk funny." I never considered that I had an accent. Me, with my mid-west accent from Illinois replied, "You think I talk funny; I think you all talk funny."

PHOTO: (L to R): Nancy, Nellie, Bob the Beekeeper, Unknown, Mrs. Preble, Neighbor, Let, Jim, Rainy. Day of the sale, May 1, 1987.

It was the family's consensus that we liked the farm and wanted to buy it. Mrs. Preble directed, "Well... We need to talk about the price." She stated her asking price and no one said anything, so without much hesitation she offered a lower price. The same thing happened again, so she lowered the price again. I kept my mouth shut. Nellie finally spoke up and said we would pay that price.

It was May 1, 1987. We bought the farm for less than three quarters of her original asking price, and her asking price was already quite low in my opinion, but I didn't know anything about Maine property values nor the value of New England farmland. We agreed on the price and tentatively agreed on a closing date.

With the deal made, everyone stepped out onto the porch to a yard full of other people. The neighbors, including the beekeeper had come to meet the new buyers. Everyone seemed happy. What we did not learn until later was that the beekeeper was there to buy the farm and even had a check for the full amount in his pocket. My mind was racing. I had just participated in a major life changing decision: Nancy and I were going to move to Maine. I was going to be a blueberry farmer.

A month before our purchase, Mrs. Preble deeded a small, 100 by 145 feet, roughly one third acre tract upon which the old Campbell School house was located to Effie Gourley who owned the schoolhouse. Effie did not own the land under it. Mr. Preble had refused to sell it to Effie as long as he was alive.

With the farm purchase behind us, we got married on Halloween, October 31, 1987. Nancy, being a frugal Mainer, was thinking my annual Halloween party should serve as our wedding reception. Both the wedding at the Glen Oak Park Arboretum and the Halloween party were a success. We spent our wedding night at Jumer's Castle Lodge.

We didn't move to Maine until I found a job. With the help of a Native Mainer friend, Fred, who gave me a list of job openings in the planning field, I found myself sitting through four job interviews in one day in August of 1987. I did Sanford first, then Lewiston, Androscoggin Valley Council of Governments (AVCOG), and Kittery last. Two were offered, one said I was overqualified, and one just wanted to see who I was as they had heard of me. That was a bit of an ego trip for me. The Town of Sanford offered to match my Peoria County salary and pay a substantial part of our moving costs. One of Sanford's Board of Selectmen owned rental property and offered us a small house on Montreal Street. We agreed to rent it sight unseen. With the moving van loaded and our cars packed and equipped with new CB radios. I locked the door on 2016 West Clarke Avenue for the last time. We left West Peoria early February 11th. We stopped at 7/11 Convenience store on Western Avenue at the end of Clarke Avenue for a couple coffees to go.

Nancy, the Planter, drove her Nova with her cat Delilah, and I, the Planner, drove my little Dodge Omni with my Scottie, McDuff. We got caught in a lake effect snowstorm near Batavia, New York. The wind was playing havoc with the 17-foot aluminum canoe tied to the roof of my car. When we stopped, Nancy was in a panic. "I think the cat died." Delilah was in a cationic trance. After we got checked into a motel Delilah came out of it. We locked the dog and cat in the bathroom while we went for dinner. The restaurant was unusual with country western decor, rock and roll music playing on the speakers and Chinese entries on the menu. When we got back to the room the smell was overpowering. Duffy had crapped from one end of the bathroom to the other. How are we going to sleep in that room? We cleaned up the mess and were so tired that sleep was not a problem. From there it was a terrifying ride. The snow was deep, and the highways were not yet completely clear. As we drove through Vermont there were cars loaded with ski racks on the roofs of their Volvos, Acuras, and Mercedes and license plates from New York, Pennsylvania and New Jersey. I wondered what they thought when they saw a little Omni with Illinois plates carrying a canoe on the roof. Have any of them tried taking a canoe down the ski slope?

We arrived in Maine on Valentine's Day in 1988 a couple days ahead of the moving van. When we arrived in Sanford, we got a motel room. The next day we drove over to see what we had rented.

We could not believe how small the house was. It was about the size of a two stall garage. As we stood looking at the house we noticed that the enclosed front porch was filled with junk and

PHOTO: 2 Montreal Street, Sanford, ME (Feb 1988).

garbage bags of stuff. To add to the angst, a shingle slid off the roof and fell onto a snowbank in front of me. It was overwhelming. We tried repeatedly to call the landlord but got no answer. Had I made a big mistake? A couple days later the landlord called to apologize. He had been out of town. A few days later, when the moving van arrived, they got out of the semi and said, "It's not going to fit." I knew they were probably right, but somehow they made everything go into the limited space. After filling the first floor and attic bedrooms, they filled the basement by stacking things from floor to ceiling and stacking things on the basement steps as they backed out. Naturally, a few things we needed were under boxes at the far end of the basement.

PHOTO: One of several gas lights in the old house at the farm.

As the new Sanford Planning Director, I found the job hectic, but I accepted the challenge. I had done well with my career thus far, so in the back of my mind was the big question, 'Can I do well in this new environment?' On Fridays, Nancy would load the car or truck with food, necessary tools, and clothes while I was at work. At five o'clock I got off work and came home to change clothes. We would point the vehicle east to Rte. 111 then head north on I-95. At Fairfield we got off the Interstate and took Rte. 201 to Skowhegan. From there it was 150 north to Brighton Road in Athens, which took us up to Rte. 16 in Mayfield before turning east toward Kingsbury. Just below the Kingsbury Dam we drove along Campbell Road in the dark for two and a half miles before finally reaching the farm. Much to our chagrin it took at least four hours to do the trip. We tried to go to the farm every weekend if the weather permitted and if there were not some other important functions we needed to attend. I would attempt to light the gas lights in the old house to put things away and to make the bed. Sometimes we would bring my old 10 x 10 foot Sears Ted Willams umbrella tent and pitch it in the front yard of the old house.

As winter arrived in 1988 we decided to buy cross country skis to get into the farm when the access road was closed for the winter. Kingsbury, much like most towns in Maine, does not plow seasonal roads in winter. It is assumed that seasonal roads are for camp lots and farms be damned. So, we each bought cross country skis and enjoyed the vast area of the farm. We also bought snowshoes for walking in the woods when the snow was deep. They were necessary when hunting for moose and deer antler drops in January and February.

Before the harvest we would keep busy cutting brush and trying to make the old house as habitable as possible. We had little to no equipment, and we had no barn to put it in even if we did. Nancy's parents, Let and Nellie, loaned us what we needed. Mrs. Preble did not have any substantial equipment either; however, she did leave us with one antique winnowing machine. The Prebles hired a neighbor to do the field mowing. What little equipment the Preble's had was stored in the old blacksmith's shop which was the size of a single stall garage with a bump out on the back. The old, hinged door on the shop was rotted, and it was a trial to open and close due to the amount of rocks and dirt swelled against it. I don't know why I

PHOTO: Allen's Freezer Plant in Ellsworth, aJer the plant moved to Hancock ME (2019). The truck is our one-ton GMC.

padlocked it because anyone who wanted to get in could simply rip the door off the hinges. The shed was chock-full of old Wyman's wooden blueberry boxes — some rotten, and some not.

We sent our blueberries to Allen's Freezer Plant in Ellsworth. The purchase of the farm was financed by Allen's at a favorable interest rate, and we thought the right thing to do was to take the berries to them (it was actually a condition of the loan). We wanted Allens to know we were serious about being blueberry farmers. We would load what we could onto our recently purchased Datsun pickup that I bought from a car dealer in Sanford near where I worked.

We would take our berries to Let and Nellie's farm in Sebec to offload the berries onto their one-ton GMC. In 1989 we bought a 1980 blue GMC, from O'Conner GMC east of Augusta.

PHOTO: A crew from the early years of harvesting.

Let, Jim and I took turns running the berries to Ellsworth in the evening. It was common for two of us to go together to keep the other awake.

Nancy used to hire a crew of 20 to 35 rakers during the harvest in August. Some were high school aged, and some were retired individuals. They were an eclectic bunch of people. Some were good rakers who could earn a decent paycheck, and then there were some who didn't make enough to pay for their gas to get to the farm. It has always been difficult to find labor for the farm due to our remote location and state restrictions on camping prohibiting us from letting people camp on site. We are not near any towns with a sizable population. A good many of them did not show up for work once the annual Skowhegan Fair opened.

We or my son, Jake, would run the winnowing machines to ensure the winnowing was done properly. In those early years we would pay the rakers by the number of boxes they filled and when it was left to them to winnow their berries the boxes were usually not completely full. A few rakers were not very good at using a rake. In other words, their berries were full of leaves and sticks. It takes more time to winnow those buckets. During the first few years Jacob would come from California to help with the harvest—help with winnowing the berries.

During Jake's 1993 visit we took him to the Roadkill Café in Greenville with menu items such as "What the UPS driver hit on his way to Greenville." I found an old decrepit 4-wheel drive International Scout in the Uncle Henry's weekly Swap or Sell It Guide. Jake and I drove to Freeport to check it out. Surprisingly, it ran. Jake liked it so I bought it, but he had to return to California before I could borrow Let's truck and trailer to pick it up. Nancy taught Jake, age twelve, how to drive a stick shift using our Datsun pickup during his summer at the farm. I thought the Scout would be a project he and I could work on when he came during future summers. However, Jake has not been back to the farm since that summer. A few years later Nancy got tired of having that piece of

PHOTO: Jacob pouring berries on to a box winnower while a raker checks the blueberry box.

junk sitting around so while I was out of state on a job related trip she gave the Scout to one of the rakers.

When a raker filled the five gallon buckets they were instructed to set them near the winnowing machine with their name box on top to keep their berries separate from other raker's berries. A 'name box' is just an upside down wooden blueberry box with masking tape on the side and the raker's name written on the masking tape. Arguments sometimes ensued because some rakers would set their berries too close to the others berries and that raker would stake claim. A watchful eye was necessary to keep order in the ranks. The berries were winnowed into the rectangular wooden boxes also called crates or flats. The boxes were then stacked with the name box on top. After the winnowing was finished it was time to total each raker's boxes and enter the number in the book so when Friday came they would be paid based on the total boxes. Covering the berries is important because the moisture in the berries evaporates quickly in the hot sun.

Early wooden blueberry boxes were pretty much square, 16-1/2 by 15-1/2 by 6 inches but that changed before we bought the farm. The boxes were reconfigured to be more of a rectangular shape at 19 inches long by 13 inches wide by 6 inches deep. The new wooden boxes had cleats on the bottom so they would not slide when stacked together. To load the truck, one person, Nancy or I, would climb up on the deck and another one or two people would carry the boxes from near the winnowing machine and place them on the truck deck. The boxes would be stacked in a fashion to minimize their shifting while driving. This often meant that a few empty boxes were set on end at the end of a row to fill up any empty deck space. It takes a while to stack 90 to 120 boxes. Once the truck was loaded the berries had to be driven to Sebec to be offloaded to the Bucks' truck or to load the Bucks' berries onto our truck. We would lay a string across the last of Buck's boxes so they would be able to separate their berries from the others when they were offloaded at the freezer plant.

At the freezer plant, the berries were weighed then fed into a giant winnowing machine then through a water bath before heading into the freezer. In the early days when delivering to the Allen's Freezer Plant in Ellsworth, as the berries entered the freezer they would drop as a curtain one berry thick by about four feet wide and perhaps about four feet tall. There was an optical scanner that would read the berries as they fell and any berry that was odd shaped or the wrong color you could hear the air jet shoot it out of the curtain. From there the berries went into boxes before going to storage.

At the peak of the season, which is usually the first two weeks of August, there was often a queue waiting for a turn to back up to the loading dock. Allen's had a crew of men that did the unloading onto

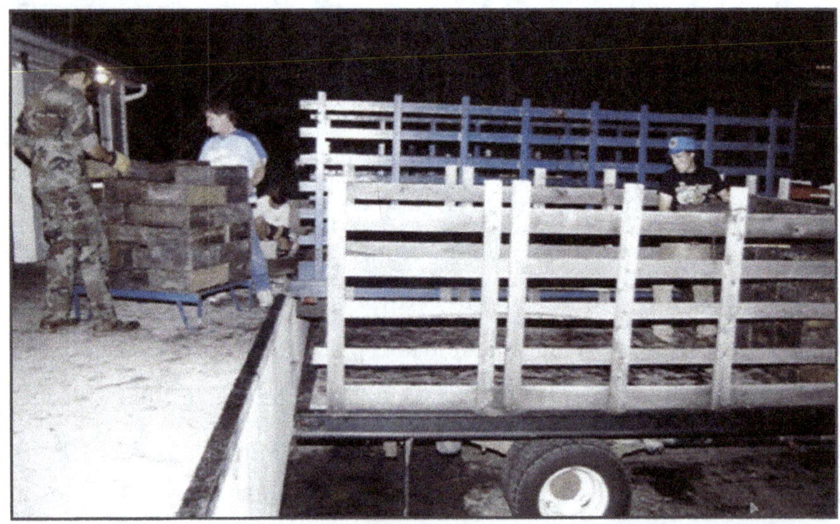

PHOTO: Unloading Let's truck at Allen's Freezer Plant in Ellsworth, ME (AUG 2000).

wooden four by four foot steel and wooden pallets before using an electric hand truck to move them to the scales. After being weighed, Jason Allen would hand me a slip of paper with the totals for this trip. Next, it was time to back up to the empty box pile and load empties onto the truck for the next load to be brought to Ellsworth. There was a man up on a higher platform grabbing the empty boxes as they came out of a hole in the wall on a conveyor from the freezer plant. His job was to look the boxes over and repair any that needed fixing, such as replacing broken bottoms or sides or re-nailing loose wood. He would then send them down to the loading area where the growers could load the empties onto their trucks.

It is a three hour drive from Kingsbury to Ellsworth, and a little longer if the trip included stopping in Sebec. It was basically a 93 mile trip one way. On the way back, the trip included a stop at McDonalds, and if Bucks' berries had been loaded on the way to Ellsworth, it meant that a load of empty boxes needed to be dropped off in Sebec before continuing to Kingsbury.

PHOTO: Jason Allen next to part of our load being weighed at the freezer plant (AUG 2000).

One very late night I was on a straight run back to Kingsbury. Jake had fallen asleep about the time we passed through Kenduskeag. I stopped at the Irving station in Dover-Foxcroft to pick up milk and ice cream. Jake woke up. I climbed up on the deck to put the groceries in one of the blueberry boxes and Jake was climbing right behind me. We both saw the nightmare at the same time. I was sickened by what I discovered. The wind had carved a "V" shape out of the middle of the load of empty boxes, and I had lost at least 20 boxes. Getting back to the farm about 1:30 AM, I woke Nancy and explained what had happened. Apparently the boxes were not stacked right and the wind caught them as I was trucking down the highway. I couldn't tell where they blew off, but I knew I was too tired to go back and look for them. Working every day from sun-up to sometimes midnight takes a toll on the body. Nancy said that she and Jake would drive the route back toward Ellsworth to look for the boxes while I caught up on some much needed sleep. The Town of Kenduskeag is considered the halfway point of the trip. Fortunately, she didn't have to go quite that far. Nancy found seven smashed boxes along Route 15 just before East Corinth about 40 miles from Kingsbury. Thankfully, it happened in the wee hours of the morning, and the traffic was light. Nancy and Jake retrieved the broken boxes and got back to the farm at around 3:00 A.M. For the next several days Jake and I kept our eyes open as we drove to and from Ellsworth but never found any more boxes.

It was the season for everything to go wrong. The Chevy truck decided to have a fit a few days later, on the way back from Ellsworth. It sounded sick, as it sputtered and coughed, and had very little power. I was convinced that it was the automatic transmission — must have been from overloading it. The truck was too sick to trust it with a full load on a 90-mile plus trip to Ellsworth. To make other arrangements for the load, I had to drive to Harmony to use a phone to call Let and Nellie. That consumed a lot of time. After a couple of days of 30 mile round trips to Harmony, we decided there must be a better way. I called a cellular phone company in Augusta. They said the farm was too far out of their normal service area, but that I could borrow a bag phone if I wanted to try it. We bought the bag phone, and much to everyone's surprise, it worked.

Having solved that problem, we decided it was time to trade the sick truck in for a different one, so we went back to O'Connor's to see if a deal could be made for another truck. In 1992, we traded for a 1988 350 V-8 GMC one ton with a dump body. I convinced O'Connor's to put a radio in the truck. At that time, it was a brown landscaping truck with a Pendle hook for trailer towing. They put on new tires, and I took it to Portland and had new oak decking installed.

Chapter 4 — Structures

The Perseverance Wild Blueberry Farm now spanning 316.5 acres, originally consisted of five homesteads with a one room school located south of the center. The schoolhouse and one of the houses still stand.

PHOTO: As the house looked in 1988.

According to Mrs. Preble, our timber frame cape-style farmhouse is approximately 190 years old. This claim is corroborated by the great-great-grandson of the original builder, Mr. Rufus Campbell.

The house is believed to have been constructed around 1835.

At one time it was attached to a walkover to a barn at the west end.

PHOTO Model T frame and engine on rock wall.

PHOTO: Old blacksmith's shop.

PHOTO: Home Clarion wood cook stove with water reservoir n right side.

PHOTO: Old blacksmith's shop.

In the early 1990's I saw a piece of metal sticking out of the ground where that original barn sat. I tried to pull it up with my hands, but it would not give. I hitched a chain to it and used the tractor to pull it out. To my amazement I pulled up a Ford Model T frame and engine. This big conversation piece now sits on a low rock wall just south of the new barn.

The small nearby shed was said to have served as a blacksmith shop when Kingsbury was in its heyday. That shed collapsed in the winter of 2016-2017. The site was cleared during the summer of 2017 and planted with grass seed.

PHOTO: Amos Cowett on his jitter bug in front of the Campbell house in 1945.

The circa 1835 farmhouse, situated at the end of a lane two tenths of a mile north of Campbell Road, has been in a state of disrepair since before we purchased the farm. The house is still standing but continues to deteriorate — the wallpaper is the only thing holding it together. The Preble family used the farmhouse as a summer residence until 1986. The first floor boasts three bedrooms, a kitchen, a parlor with a Home Atlantic wood stove, a table, and chairs, and a stairway leading to the attic between the two eastern bedrooms and

PHOTO: The kitchen as it looked in 1988.

the parlor. The kitchen floor has a severe slant of approximately one foot drop in ten. On one side of the kitchen is a Home Clarion wood stove with a copper-lined hot water reservoir on the right side. It is said that Mr. Preble purchased this new stove in Addison, Maine, in

PHOTO: Parlor Home Atlantic Parlor Stove.

1914 when he married his first wife, 23 year old Mable who died in 1942 at the age of 51.

At the north end of the house is a pantry with a countertop, two burner gas stove and a Servel gas refrigerator in a back corner. A door in the back northwest corner of the kitchen led to the woodshed and 'indoor' privy. A porcupine assumed residence under that end of the house and proceeded to eat the outhouse. Yes, it likes the salty

PHOTO: Kingsbury Plantation, Maine, Ames Cowett house and barn, 1945.

wood, and in the severe winter weather it beats going out into the cold woods. The attic walls were last covered with newspapers dated in the 1890's.

The attic was a treasure trove of abandoned farm paraphernalia such as rusted bed frames, old baskets, jars, hand sprayers, and the like, most of which have been removed. There were two unfinished and one finished bedroom in the attic. The sills and floor joists, as well as much of the remainder of the structure have rotted. We used the house until November 1999 during hunting season. That same year I increased the number of floor supports from three to seven. As I tightened the screw jacks, the floor joists compressed and crunched under the pressure. All seven jacks fell over within the course of a few weeks. The old house is now too tired to provide shelter.

Up behind the Campbell House to the northeast was the Cowett homestead. Cowett Hill was named after the Cowett family who lived in a house a little more than one hundred yards south from the top of the hill. It was a weather-beaten, one-and-a-half story wood frame structure resting on field stone cellar walls. The gable ends faced north and south; a kitchen wall ran to the east; and just beyond that was the large barn. Just south of the house was a chicken shed. To the east of the barn was a dug well. Amos Cowett lived in this home with his wife, Avis May (Ward), four sons, Shirley, Leone, Rodney, and Levi and two daughters, Betty and Clair. I initially thought 'Shirley' was an odd name for a boy but have since learned that it was not that uncommon in Maine.

Shirley and Levi frequented the farm during blueberry harvest but always came separately. I encouraged both to come visit together and tell us what life was like when they lived at the farm. They agreed and on a Sunday in September of 2002 they visited us. Nancy and I spent the day walking the farm with Shirley and Levi, listening to them reach back to the early 1940's. Life was not easy for the Cowetts as Kingsbury was quite remote and beyond the electric company's reach. The grocery truck came every Tuesday and area residents would buy groceries off the truck and/or place orders for items not sold on the truck. Those items would be delivered the following Tuesday. The mail truck came about every other day to pick up the blueberries. It was a one-ton truck with a box body. Levi's son and wife came to the farm with him to rake blueberries. Levi used to rake back when Mr. Preble was living. He told Nancy that Mr. Preble used to take afternoon naps and carried candy in his pocket. When a raker did an excellent job raking or one of the boys would help move the winnowing machine Mr. Preble would reward them with a piece of candy.

Amos was the provider and head of the household. He worked in the woods in the fall and winter, and the family had a substantial garden. And of course, there were blueberries. Most of the fields were hay fields but there was only one blueberry field on the part of the farm they owned, which was north of Campbell Road, That field was at the far north end of the farm on the east side of the lane going back to the woods. In early August when the blueberries ripened, the boys would rake the berries to provide the family with a little extra cash for school supplies and clothes. Levi recalled that one year they had to rake enough blueberries to pay to have his tonsils removed. They did not own livestock but did have two work horses. Shirley could not remember what was planted but remembered that the horse that pulled the plow would stop and refuse to go. Levi remembered that he and his siblings would throw rocks at the horse to get it moving again. Shirley told of a time when there was so much snow that their car got stuck near the bend in Campbell Road where it takes a 90-degree turn from south to east, about a mile up from Kingsbury Pond. The old man that lived in a farmhouse on the corner of the bend hitched his team of horses to the car and pulled it all the way up to the old Cowett house about another mile and half. The old man wore no shoes and trudged through the deep snow with just thick wool socks.

To provide food for the family table, Amos would often hunt for deer and other meat. He was somewhat infamous for jacklighting deer (jacking deer) — that is, hunting deer at night with a rifle and flashlight. It was illegal then as it is now. You may have heard the expression "froze like a deer in the headlights." A bright flashlight will do the same to a deer as the car's headlights. It makes it easier for the hunter to take aim and kill the animal. The game warden who also ran the Wagon Wheel Restaurant based in Abbot, was determined to catch Amos in the act of jacking deer. Every time there was a dusting of snow, the warden would drive to Kingsbury and try to track Amos. He never caught him.

One late September night in 1945, Amos and a couple of his buddies went out with their rifles and flashlights to the north side of State Route 16 that traverses Kingsbury. One of his friends shined his flashlight on what he thought were a deer's eyes and pulled the trigger. Unfortunately, Amos was wearing a rhinestone belt buckle that night and when the light struck the flashy rhinestones, the shooter thought it was the deer's eyes. Amos bled to death before they could drive him

Harmony Tribute

Volume 2, Number 9   HARMONY, MAINE, OCTOBER, 1945   Price, 10 Cents Per Copy

Maple Farm Home Destroyed By Fire

Maple Farm, the home of Lyman (Red) Wentworth, the former Henry Marble place, caught fire on the afternoon of September 16. The fire started in the barn. Arlene and three small children were alone at home, since Mrs. Wentworth was visiting their daughter and Mr. Wentworth was working in the woods. Arlene threw a pail of water on the fire but seeing it was rapidly spreading she ran to the woods for her father. It was a windy day and the buildings, including a new barn were completely destroyed. A bull, tractor, 100 tons of hay, farm machinery, grain and most of the furniture were burned. Sparks alighted on Irving Braley's garage causing some damage. Mr. Wentworth estimates that the insurance will cover about one-third of the loss. At the present the family is living with Merrill Annis. Ernest Wentworth has been called to go in the Navy October 4, but if he can remain at home until the middle of October the family plans to start a new home this fall on the old foundation.

Lt. Walter Raleigh Is Transferred

Second Lt. Walter Raleigh, USAAC, son of Chief Officer Alonzo Raleigh and Mrs. Raleigh Seabury, recently has been transferred from Greenville, Miss., to Craig Field, Selma, Ala., for further training as a pilot. A graduate of Harmony high school in 1935, he was employed at the Portsmouth Navy Yard from 1939 until he entered service in October, 1942. He has had training in New Jersey, Colorado, Tennessee, and Florida and received his wings at Craig Field in February, 1944. He has since been an instructor at Greenville.

There are four members of the family in the service. Lt. (jg) Harry S. Raleigh, USCG, enlisted as a surfman in December, 1936, and was stationed at Cross Island, Brant Rock, Mass., and was acting captain of the port at Plymouth, Mass., for a year. After working for a time in the main office of the Coast Guard in Boston, he studied navigation at St. Augustine, Fla., and went to sea in March, 1944. According to information received by his parents, he had an active part in the retaking of the Philippine Islands. His wife and son, Harry Jr., live in San Francisco, Calif.

The youngest son of the Raleighs, Roland Raleigh, shipfitter 1/c, USNR, left his work as welder at the Portsmouth Navy Yard to enter the service two years ago this month. After boot training at Newport, R. I., he was stationed at Norfolk, Va., and went overseas in February of last year. He is stationed at present in the Solomon Islands. A graduate of Lubec high school in 1940, he studied engineering for a time at the University of New Hampshire and later worked at the South Portland shipyard.

Like many other York fathers, Chief Raleigh is repeating in this war the work he did in World War I as a member of the maritime service. He enlisted in January, 1944, and is stationed on the Atlantic coast. Formerly owner of a store in Harmony, he was employed at the navy yard from 1939 until last year. He is a member of the South Portland lodge of Masons.

KINGSBURY MAN KILLED BY NIGHT HUNTING COMPANION IN MIXUP

Amos Cowette, 35, of Kingsbury, father of six children, died about 11 o'clock Friday night, September 28, in a Dover-Foxcroft hospital as the result of a hunting accident involving a hunting companion, George P. Giles, also of Kingsbury.

* * * * * * * * * *

CHRISTMAS OVERSEAS ISSUE NEXT MONTH

The November issue of the Tribute will be the overseas Christmas edition carrying Greeting Cards to the men in the service.

These Greeting Cards, costing 25 cents for six lines, should be given to Mrs. Rita Reed in Harmony, Mrs. Ray Tibbetts in Athens, Mrs. Verner Curtis in Wellington, and Mrs. Charles Leader in Cambridge before October 20th.

The boys cannot be home for Christmas so let's all do the next best thing by greeting them thru the columns of the Tribute—their own little paper.

* * * * * * * * * *

According to the officials investigating the incident, Giles and Cowette started out hunting late Friday afternoon with guns and flashlights, Giles carrying a single-barrel 12 gauge and having four of the five shells loaded with buckshot. These officials said that Giles told them that after dark he thought he saw eyes some distance away, that he thought Cowette was behind him and focusing his light on what he thought were the eyes of a deer, he fired his gun. Cowette called out that he had been shot and when Giles reached him, he was half sitting and half lying on the ground, the officials said.

Giles asked his companion if he was hurt badly, the officials said, and Cowette replied that he did not think so but that his legs were numb. Giles then went for help and Cowette was later removed to the Dover-Foxcroft hospital where he succumbed to his injuries later that night.

Discharged From Service

Cpl. Edwin Cuddy has been discharged from the service after serving two years overseas. He served in Africa, Sicily and Italy with Gen. Mark Clark's Fifth Army. Corporal Cuddy was inducted December 20, 1942, going to Camp Lee, Virginia, for his basic training and leaving for overseas in May, 1943. He was awarded the Good Conduct Medal, Badge Driver-W, and the ETO Ribbon with four Campaign Stars. Cpl. Edwin Cuddy is staying with his wife and little daughter Simone at the home of Mr. and Mrs. Myron Russell.

Happy Though Married

I have often wondered how many young fellows will remember that sacred moment when he turned away from the preacher and walked back down the aisle with his wife. In the matter of a few moments I became an entirely

(continued on page 2)

PHOTO: Newspaper article regarding hunting accident when Amos Cowett was shot.

to the Mayo Hospital in Dover-Foxcroft about 25 miles east. Amos was 35 at the time of his death. Shirley was eleven and Levi was only three when their father died.

Due to the loss of their head of household, the family decided to sell their farm in 1952. Levi and his wife still frequent the farm for a visit and to rake blueberries.

On the north end of the farm is a cellar hole, and east and west of it is a large rock wall that was once the True Ames homestead. There is also a clump of trees now surrounding the former foundation. At several hundred feet east of the cellar hole is a large gathering of

PHOTO: Barn built in 1993. Photo taken in 2012.

rocks marking the location of the Ames barn. We found the apparent four corners of the structure. It is a New England tradition to build outbuildings as close as possible to the house. Winter weather was the main reason. Some individuals died getting lost in the blizzard when trying to tend to their critters in the barn. Mr. Ames barn defied this rule and placed his barn almost 100 yards from the main house, but we don't know why.

On the far south end of the farm is another cellar hole and west of it is a large wall of rocks that was a barn foundation. This was the homestead of the Curtis family. They settled here from Massachusetts. Near this feature is another small hole closer to the south property line. Decades ago, it was a shallow pit that was the source of slate for the students at the Campbell School.

Nancy's father, Let, told us that if we built a barn, he would loan us a tractor to use for mowing the fields. We researched the ads for pole buildings and found an ad for a pole barn at Wickes Lumber. We drove to their facility in Fairfield and started discussing our needs with the man behind the counter. He told me he knew a dairy farmer that could build us a better pole barn for roughly the same cost. That sounded good to me. We met with the farmer, and we agreed on a 48' x 40' barn to be built. It had a 50 pound snow load metal roof supported with 2" x 4" prefab trusses, shiplap siding, four horizontal sliding windows down each side, and a four inch thick concrete floor. As the guy was getting ready to set the forms for the floor, I told him I wanted the dirt floor compacted before it was poured. I could tell he wasn't entirely happy about my demand. He said if it sat in the open for a few rain showers it should be okay. I wanted it to be compacted with a vibrating compactor. He agreed.

There are two large ten foot high overhead garage doors at either end of the structure, and one pedestrian door on the north end. The barn was finished in September 1993. The next spring, I noticed the north gable end was splitting and the bottom of the north wall was a few inches above the concrete floor. I called the farmer and asked him how deep he set the posts. He said four feet. I reminded him that I had asked him to set them at six feet. He replied that he always set them at four feet and never had any problem.

I told him this was Kingsbury, and we are at a higher elevation and further north than Fairfield. He came up to look at the situation and concluded there was not much he could do other than start over and he didn't want to do that. He made little profit on this project. I did not want to hurt the man financially. I had already given him my displeasure of getting paint all over my Honda generator when he used it to spray paint the barn. I felt sorry for the guy. We got a good deal on the barn at less than $20,000. Perhaps, it was partially my fault for not digging a deeper swale around the north end to better drain the water before it got too close to the barn. Over the next few decades, the north end continued to heave higher. At this point there isn't much that can be done. I have had a couple of contractors look at it, and they both said it is best to just leave it alone unless I want to spend more than I paid for the barn in the first place.

We spent more time discussing the stain color than we did deciding all the other features combined. We originally decided on Cape Cod Gray but in later years changed to a gray cottonwood stain. In 2024, I decided to do the third repaint and did the trim around the windows and the garage doors in a yellow cottonwood stain. A close friend and one of my hunting buddies donated a large cast iron wood stove that sits in the northwest corner and my brother-in-law hitched up a stack in 1999.

Also, in 1999 we decided we were ready to build a new house. The first step was to select an appropriate site. At first, Nancy wanted to build a house on top of the hill near where her sunset rock is. I objected to that purely on the grounds that I was not going to plow snow from Campbell Road all the way to the top of the hill. First it would involve buying a plow truck, and second, I didn't want to spend hours plowing and then maintaining the equipment needed to accomplish that chore. My third argument was I didn't think we could get a permit to put a septic tank and a well on top of all the ledges. Nancy finally agreed. We wanted a view but that would be too expensive. We finally settled on a site less than halfway up the hill from the old house. We bought the house plans for a modified Cape Cod style building, hired a site evaluator, and had a septic system designed and staked out. While all of this was going on, I was experiencing a lot of pain in my right shoulder, neck, and arm.

Finally in August of 2000 I had surgery to fuse a couple of vertebrae in my neck along with the removal of a few significant bone spurs on my spine that were pinching several nerves. This set us back. We knew we couldn't continue using the old house for fear it may cave in with us in it. We went to a manufactured housing show at the Augusta Civic Center, and we decided that a mobile home might be a temporary answer to our need for a place to stay when working at the farm.

PHOTO: The Sidell's mobile home at 421 Campbell Road.

Now this was a major step for me. As the former Peoria County Planning and Zoning director the county was extremely critical of mobile homes. The county still assumed then that mobile homes provided substandard housing that deteriorated and depreciated rapidly. Yet there I was buying one for my own use. We ordered a 14' x 70' with two bedrooms, two bathrooms, dining room, living room and kitchen, unfurnished. Much to my surprise, I liked it… level floors, weather tight, new and spacious.

We decided that we did not want it near the barn and the old house. For some reason we thought it would conflict with the traditional image we had of the farm. The other reason is that it would not be readily accessible in the winter since Preble Lane is considered a seasonal road and is not open during the winter. Therefore, we decided to put it on the south side of the farm. An additional benefit of this location was a drilled well where Mr. Preble's son used to park his Airstream in the summer just south of Campbell Road and west of the schoolhouse. We chose a place 150 feet off Campbell Road and near the west edge of the south fields. We had hired Wynn Herrick to do the site work of getting the area leveled, installing the septic tank, and running a line from the drilled well to the new site. It took several truckloads of fill to create a large enough area for the long structure and to bring the driveway into the site. The unit was delivered near the end of October. The roof of the mobile home rode higher than that of the pickup trucks that travel Campbell Road and consequently it broke off many tree branches on the way to the farm. It didn't suffer too badly from all the tree collisions. It was dropped parallel to the driveway but not up to the site.

I called the dealer to ask when they would come to set it up. I was told they would contact their contract person and tell him we were ready. I waited over a week with no activity. I called again, and again, and finally, I got in contact with the man who was hired to set the unit. He was a surly individual and was not inclined to do the work any time soon. I pressed and he finally said he would do it. We did not hit it off well. He bitched and I complained, and I found out he had not wanted to do the job because he was busy hunting. He hitched the unit to his big truck and proceeded to back it up to the site. He made several attempts but could not get up the slight grade. He then told me he blew a hydraulic line and had to quit. We exchanged words and I told him he was an acerbic recalcitrant jerk of an individual. He was taken aback. While I regretted my quick temper fearing he might want to pick a fight, anger won over. He said he was going to look up those words. I doubted he would remember them by the time he got back to Bangor. Thankfully, Wynne Herrick's son, Travis, was working the woods with his skidder not too far from us. We asked if he could push the mobile home onto the site for us. He came with the skidder and in one quick try he perfectly got the unit exactly in line with the blocks, water and septic lines. We were all amazed at how he did it. He had never tried to set up a mobile home before, and he surprised himself. I guess it came down to all the years of moving logs and forestry equipment in tight spaces of the woods that gave him the edge.

On December 2, 2000, Nancy and I were sitting in our new 'traylah' and she cried out, "Look out the window!" There it was: the first time I saw a wild turkey. Then another. That was the beginning of the Turkey War. They eat blueberries in addition to everything else.

We hired a plumber to hitch up the water, install two surge tanks and hook the drainpipes to the septic system. We were fortunate to have a drilled well (211 feet deep) nearby, so we didn't have that added expense. As it was, we had to run an underground insulated water line approximately 65 feet to the mobile home.

Within a year, I built a 10-foot by 10-foot platform for a metal $299 Sears' garden shed to house the generator that supplies power to the mobile home. It is fifteen feet east of the mobile home. We used our 5,000 watt old gas powered Honda generator to supply electricity. I tried to insulate the metal shed with one inch Styrofoam by gluing the pieces to the interior of the metal walls. That lasted for a couple of months before the Styrofoam began falling off. Having

PHOTO: Deck of the mobile home.

gotten tired of filling the small gas tank on the generator in all kinds of weather, we invested in a liquid petroleum (LP) Honda 6500 watt unit. It is certainly much more convenient, particularly in the cold months. Now, I can flip a switch from inside the mobile home then push a button and we have electricity.

A couple of years later we hired two guys from Skowhegan to build a six-foot by ten-foot deck to replace our fiberglass steps. The deck sits in front of the sliding glass doors on the south side of the unit. I stained it redwood which now has become an annual chore. The mobile home was meant to be a temporary set up and yet 25 years later we are still using it and liking it.

Chapter 5 — Trees, Soils & Plants

With over 216 acres of woods, there are a few trees of special significance on the farm. One of the most prominent ones is at the end of the field when you first drive up the lane to the old house. It is a gnarly old apple tree. The apples are quite tart, but the deer love them.   Just beyond that field, near the elbow in the road is a huge white birch. Sadly, the rigors of severe wind have shortened the

PHOTO: Birch tree at elbow near entrance to farm.

height, but it is a survivor. On the inside corner of the elbow is a beautiful balsam fir. It was a very young tree when we bought the farm and Nancy's father told us to cut it down. We never got around to it. It now stands tall and stately. There is a row of Norway Pines along the lane that goes around the old house and up the hill. These trees were also young when we bought the farm but have grown substantially since. I am waiting for the opportunity to shoot the porcupine that has been feasting on them in the winter. Sadly, in the past two years three of these trees have died due to excessive gnawing by the porcupine.

PHOTO: Apple tree at elbow north of the Apple Tree Field.

At my son's behest, I did consider using a lone spruce tree on top of the hill that appeared to be growing out of a large rock as the farm logo. But again, Maine weather and wind robbed us of that idea. A rock with a small stump doesn't make for a good looking logo. It just did not persevere.

PHOTO: Balsom Fir at entrance elbow.

In 1999 we planted a small orchard west of the barn. There are five rows of young fruit trees as follows: 10 apple, 4 peach, 3 pear, 4 apricot, 4 plum and 2 mulberry. Nancy tried to talk me out of the mulberry, but I have fond childhood memories of a mulberry tree in the neighborhood where I grew up in central Illinois. I would pick enough mulberries so that my mom could bake a mulberry pie. Some of the trees in the orchard did not survive the first winter and the only tree to produce fruit was one of the peach trees. We canned 80 pints of peaches that year but the next year that tree also died. Nancy planted a McIntosh apple tree a couple of years later in the orchard. After a couple more years it finally started producing tiny apples. There is hope.

Nancy and her dad transplanted two apple trees north of the barn and they are high producers of gnarly apples that the deer

PHOTO: Two apple trees planted by Nancy and her father.

enjoy. Sadly, the porcupines love these trees as well, but they haven't killed them yet. They do keep them pruned. There were already several other apple trees on the farm. In addition to the two mentioned above there is a huge old apple tree on the west edge of the field where we planted the orchard. Nancy saved several young wild apple trees along the former road that went up to the old Cowett homestead. The last one worth mentioning is near the old True Ames homestead in the farm's north fields. There are no apple trees on our property south of Campbell Road. However, there is one just behind the old schoolhouse that is not ours. In the woods we have a good variety of north Maine woods' trees. However, there are no oaks. We do have balsam fir, black spruce, birch (gray, white and yellow), cedar, hemlock, mountain ash, pin cherry, red maple, red pine, red/white spruce, sugar maple, tamarack, white ash, poplar, white pine, and lots of beech. Most of the beech trees are diseased as are most beeches in Maine. In the late 2010's I planted a couple of oak seedlings near the mobile home from the massive oak tree in our

PHOTO: Lady Slipper (protected).

Oakland house front yard. They lasted about 10 years before dying. For the first few years we would cut our own Christmas tree, but after we moved to Guilford, we bought a very tall, beautiful, realistic,

PHOTO: Bracken Ferns in summer.

artificial tree. This meant we no longer had to trek through the snow pulling a sled, all for a real tree.

Our stand of wood is not as healthy as we would like. This is due in part to extensive harvesting in the 1950's and 1970's. Since then, the woods have never been properly thinned. Unfortunately, many of the beech trees are infected with a bark disease and since 2021 a beech leaf disease has been detected in all Maine counties. Beech nuts are a dietary staple for deer and bears. Some naturalists are quite concerned about Maine's future black bear population since this bark disease is statewide. There are not many disease resistant beech on the farm.

We have contracted with Sappi Paper Mill in Skowhegan, Maine, to harvest some pulp and as a result we have developed a forest management plan that has to be updated periodically. In addition to pulp, some of the wood goes for lumber, firewood, and some clear wood goes for veneer. There is usually several years between timber harvests on the various sections of our woods.

PHOTO: Wild Iris.

PHOTO: Lupines in June.

In our woods and in the blueberry fields there are an amazing number of different plants. We have black berries, blueberries (both sour tops and low sweets), brackens (and other ferns), bristly sarsaparilla, British soldier moss, bunch berries, chickweed, clover, grass, dandelions, fire weed, golden rod, Indian hemp, Japanese knotweed (bamboo), lady slippers (protected), lupines, milkweed, raspberries, sedge grass, St. John's wort, trilliums (stinking Benjamins, and painted trilliums), Virginia creeper, wild iris, wild oats, wild strawberries, winter berry, yellow and orange hawkweed (devil's paintbrush), and of course, many more.

PHOTO: Bracken Ferns in Fall.

Bunch berries are a serious problem. They can be eaten raw or cooked but they have an extremely hard large seed in their center. One could break a tooth on it if it was in your blueberry pie or muffin. They grow closer to the ground and can be difficult to avoid when raking the blueberries.

PHOTO: British Soldier Lichen.

PHOTO: Lichen.

PHOTO Sour-top Blueberries ready for harvest in August.

PHOTO: Crocus.

PHOTO: *Winter berries.*

Chapter 6 — Water and Wells

We have several wells on the farm. There is a drilled well approximately 60 feet northeast of the mobile home site. It is approximately 211 feet deep and was on site when we bought the farm. The well was drilled by Haskell Well Drilling out of Sangerville, Maine in 1981. It was originally drilled to serve an Airstream travel trailer placed on the farm each summer by Mr. Preble's son who came up from Georgia during the harvest. He also had a makeshift steel barrel 'septic system.'

PHOTO: *Hand pump on dug well in front of old house, 2003.*

There are also three dug wells on the farm. One lies between the house and the old blacksmith's shop. It is stone lined and estimated to be 25 feet deep. In the spring it is usually brim full, but by August it is nearly dry. I built a new well cover and installed a red cast iron hand pump (made in China) over the well in 1995. It worked for only one season but remained for years for aesthetic reasons. I built this well cover and added the pump because I was hosting a national Association of State Floodplain Managers in Portland and had set up a farm tour at the end of the conference. Water from this well was used for washing dishes and during blueberry season we rigged up a small wading pool with a shower curtain hanging from a wagon wheel rim that was attached to the ceiling in the back bedroom of the old house. We had a black two and a half gallon shower bag that was laid on the well cover for the sun to heat. At times it was too hot for comfort.

A second dug well is on the south slope of Cowett Hill directly uphill from the old farmhouse. The Preble's had buried a water line from this well to the house for gravity flow water. We seldom hitch it up because the water level is generally low in August when we most need it.

The third well is east of the old Cowett cellar hole. It is the most reliable of the dug wells, although not as deep. It was often used to fill the sprayer tank during times when it was needed to mix and spray insecticide and fungicides. We stopped using this well in 2000 after we hitched up the drilled well to serve the mobile home.

There are also three springs on the farm. The closest one is just southwest of the barn. It feeds a large wetland south of it. It also dries up in August. There is another along the west property line that has a pond about the size of a bedroom. It does not appear to dry up during the summer. On the far northwest corner of the farm is the third, small spring and it is very susceptible to drying up during any dry spell.

All the wells and springs are full in the early spring due to snow melting and spring rains. Unfortunately, the dug wells and springs usually dry up in late summer.

Chapter 7 — Wildlife

The Kingsbury area is rich in wildlife: we have a large diversity of critters. The biggest, of course, is the moose. The moose are seen more frequently than the white-tailed deer, although we do have a lot of deer here, too. It is not uncommon to have a moose trek across the field in the morning fog when we are running the winnowing

PHOTO: *Momma Moose and her twins in the mobile home dooryard,* 2002.

machine. They may stop to look but then wander off to the other side of the field and disappear into the woods, or they may seek out a pond to escape the heat. It is rare to see them out in the fields on bright sunny days. They prefer to stay in the woods when it is hot. When I first started deer hunting on the farm, it was routine for a couple of years that as I entered the woods on the northeast part of the farm each morning, I would encounter a large bull moose with huge shovels standing just inside the woods line. I would stop and it would turn his massive head to look at me. I would talk to him, and he just stood there. Eventually, one of us would walk away after a couple of minutes. This only occurred for a couple of years, but there is moose poop all along the wood's trails, even today. In the early 2000's there was a momma moose that seemed to have twins every other year. She would walk out of the woods and cross the dooryard next to the mobile home. She never hurried; she was just looking for somewhere to browse.

As the Maine State National Flood Insurance Coordinator, I was asked to host a meeting of the Community Rating System in Portland many years ago. A couple of the FEMA members asked if I could take them to see a moose, if time permitted. I agreed and invited them to the farm. I had planned to take them on the Golden Road, which was usually a good place to see moose. They all came to the farm the night before, and we had a good evening of conversation. They drank all of my wine. Early the next morning at around 5:00 AM, I heard one of them open the door and go outside. After some time, I did not hear him come back in. This was in October, and the temperature was below freezing. I got up to check on things and there in the dooryard was momma and her twins browsing. I woke up the other guest, and they got to see the moose up close. I took pictures of the event and included one on our annual end-of-the-year collage of farm pictures. A few months later I got a call from one of the ladies at FEMA headquarters in Washington, D.C.

"Lou, I have a copy of the moose on your farm on the wall of my cubical. Did you take that picture?"

"Well, yes I did."

PHOTO: Red squirrel.

"Did you look at that picture?"

"Of course, I took it."

"Momma Moose and her twins. What is Momma doing? Did you see that momma moose was peeing?"

I looked at a copy at my desk, "Nope, I didn't notice that. Welcome to Maine."

Skunks seem to be everywhere in Maine. One year, early in our ownership, Nancy and our friend Bruce discovered a dead skunk in the dug well in front of the old house. With some effort they managed to lower a five gallon bucket down the well to capture the dead critter and cart the body off into the woods. As the weekend came to a close and it came time to go back to Oakland, we loaded the truck and headed south. About halfway home we smelled a powerful skunk odor. I assumed that I hit one on the road. A little later the smell permeated the cab again. It turns out that Maggie, our Scottie, had eaten some of the dead skunk and was passing skunk farts. Maggie got sick and it was a terrible mess. It reminded us of Duffy who got into the compost pile when we were living in Springvale and delivered chunks of corn cobs about two in the morning in the corner of the tent when we were camping on the front lawn of the old house a few years earlier. That dog would eat anything.

There are black bears, and we were told they shot seven bears on our farm the year before we bought it. In the span of 37 years, I have only seen a bear three times, but the fields are heavy with bear scat along the edges during the annual harvest. Bears love blueberries and can eat an acre a night. They gorge themselves and eat until they puke. They eat the blueberries to fatten up before denning for the winter sleep. In November of 1998, while deer hunting, I heard a lot

PHOTO: *Tree frog.*

of racket just north of where I was standing. I thought it was a huge moose crashing through the woods. Nope. Suddenly, I spotted a big black bear running past me, heading south. My guess is that a hunter may have scared it. The season for bears coincides with deer hunting.

I was removing rocks with the excavator one summer on the south end of the farm. Unfortunately, I threw a track (the rubber tracks that enable the machine to move). I did not have my tools with me to repair it, so I started walking up Preble Lane to the barn to fetch my toolbox. About half-way up the lane, I spotted a large black bear crossing the road in front of me. There were only a few yards between us. We both stopped. We looked at each other and fortunately the bear continued on its way. I will admit, as I walked on to the barn, I turned around several times to make sure it was not following me. There are also beaver, bobcats (rare), chipmunks, coyotes, foxes, porcupines, and raccoons. We had a family of raccoons that took up residence in the kitchen chimney of the old

PHOTO: *Snapping Turtle.*

house. We also have meadow voles, pine martens (first seen in the fall of 1999), rabbits, snowshoe hare, skunks, stoats (first seen in 2020), noisy red squirrels, snapping turtles and wood turtles, white-footed mice, and tree frogs. There are also small garter snakes, but there are no poisonous snakes in Maine. We have cedar wax wings that eat apple blossoms, white-throated sparrows, bluebirds, bluejays, chimney swifts, harrier hawks, hermit thrush (Nancy's favorite), hummingbirds, killdeer, ravens, mourning doves, owls, pileated woodpeckers, grouse or partridges, robins, finches, and my least favorite birds — turkeys. Turkeys eat blueberries even before the berries turn blue.

As I mow the fields in the fall, I mow in a counterclockwise fashion around the field. As I progress, I see the furry little meadow voles scurrying towards the center of the field. When I finally reach the center the little critters scramble in a starburst of activity across the freshly mowed ground. In the early 1990's I would jump off the tractor, after putting it in park, to pick up a vole and put it in my pocket. We would take a couple of them home to put in a large Habitrail system of colorful plastic tubes and exercise wheels along a couple of walls in our dining room. We gave them plenty of grass, cedar chips, food and water and watched them through the cold winter months. In the spring we would take them back to the farm and turn them loose. The voles and mice are a food source for the fox, coyotes, and northern harrier hawks. It is fascinating to watch the hawks cruise low over the fields as I am mowing.

Chapter 8 — Insects

PHOTO: Bumble bee on lupine.

PHOTO: *Rare engorged tick.*

What would life be like if we did not have bugs? Bees are necessary not only for the pollination of blueberries but also for any plant that flowers. We have honeybees and wild bumble bees. Other natural pollinators include moths, butterflies, wasps, and yes, even black flies. We also have a lot of other insects, some beneficial and some detrimental. We have ants, cabbage moths, caterpillars, daddy long legs, devil's darning needles, deer flies, moose flies, dragon flies, house flies, lady bugs, Luna moths, Monarch butterflies, mosquitoes, and Japanese beetles, as well as various other kinds of .

beetles, spiders (including brown jumping spiders and my favorite spider—the shamrock orb-weaver), ticks (both dog ticks and deer ticks), tent worms, red-striped fireworms, and whiteface wasps. It would be a huge task to try to list and identify all the insects, so I won't do that. I think you get the picture—lots of bugs.

Shamrock orb-weavers are beneficial. In 37 years of having them climb all over me, I have never been bitten. They eat insects and they seem to like height. I know it creeps customers out to see these spiders with a large greenish or orangish abdomen, striped legs, and little toenails climbing their way up to my neck to get on top of my hat. It bothers me to see a customer swat and kill one because of their fear of spiders. These little critters help keep the other insects in check.

PHOTO: White-faced Wasp.

PHOTO: Shamrock Orb-Weaver.

Chapter 9 — Weather

Kingsbury Plantation has a humid, continental climate, with warm summers and cold winters. Average temperatures during the summer months of June, July and August range from the mid-60's to low 80's Fahrenheit, while winter temperatures in December, January and February usually average between 20 to 35 degrees Fahrenheit.

PHOTO: Root wad from a blowdown.

We have found over the years that the temperature at the farm was usually about three to five degrees cooler than it was at our old house in Oakland. We have found the same difference to be true now that we live in Guilford. Over the past thirty years the wind has become more incessant, and much stronger. We have been experiencing more blowdowns in the woods. A couple of years ago I bought an anemometer for Nancy's birthday, and it seems to spin constantly.

The normal temperature at the farm ranges from 13.3 degrees Fahrenheit, the lowest average temperature for January, to an average of 66.6 degrees in July. This is based on the closest station being in Dover-Foxcroft, Maine, approximately 30 miles east of Kingsbury. We have experienced cold temperatures at more than 20 degrees below zero in our south fields in January and August heat waves in the upper 90's for several days.

The normal annual precipitation is 43.42 inches with November being the wettest month at 4.49 inches and February the driest at 2.93 inches. The mean annual snowfall at the farm is approximately 100 inches. April into May brings what is known in Maine as Mud Season. I have gotten myself into some real predicaments over the years. The first year we moved here, I pulled over to let a van pass on Campbell Road at the farm. As I was pulling over, Nancy started yelling "No! No Stop!" It was too late. I got Nancy's Nova caught deep in mud on the edge of the road. The van driver did not realize Campbell Road was a dead end. It wasn't long before he came back and fortunately he stopped. He said he could not pull the car out with the van, but he would give us a lift into Abbot. As he drove, his very young son in the back seat kept hitting him in the head with a fishing pole. The expletives flew and his wife was yelling at him as well. What a joyful ride. He dropped us off at Titcomb's General Store at the junction of Rt. 16 and 15. The store clerk allowed us to use the store's phone to call for a tow truck. This was before cell phones. It was late Sunday afternoon, and no one answered our several calls to various towing companies. Finally, the clerk suggested I ask a customer who had just pulled in. He had a pickup truck.

The man was a guy of few words but was willing to give us a lift back to the car and to try to pull us out. Before we could get into his truck cab, he had to throw a few dozen beer cans piled from the truck floor to the bottom of the dashboard into the back of his truck.

PHOTO: Fire truck stuck in ditch.

His young daughter, I'm guessing around two or three years old, was skeptical of the two strangers that were going to ride in her truck. She sat next to her dad and Nancy sat on my lap. There was a brief conversation about his house getting flooded the year before during the April Fool's Day Flood. I had mentioned I worked with flooding issues, and he let me know his opinion about FEMA. It was not a good conversation topic when you are asking someone to help you. When we got back to the car he hitched up a chain and pulled us out with no problem. I offered fifty dollars for his trouble, but he

PHOTO: Fire truck stuck in ditch.

refused. I offered a twenty for some beer and he accepted. Moral of the story: Don't pull onto a gravel shoulder in mud season.

A few years later when we were burning the fields, I drove the 1954 GMC pumper firetruck loaded with 500 gallons of water into a ditch along Preble Lane and sunk the right side of the truck. Let ordered, "Just leave it!" I managed to dig it out with a spade later in the day. I discovered a large boulder had gotten lodged between the rear dual wheels that most likely caused the truck to veer to the ditch.

In May of 2011, I had the bright idea of mowing the lawn early for the first time that season. I got too close to a drainage swale, and I got the Husqvarna riding mower stuck. I did not consider it to be a big problem. I went for the John Deere 4120 with four-wheel drive to pull it out. It sunk even deeper into the mud. What was I thinking?

Mud Season is a problem. In the end I got it out by placing logs and boards under the tractor's wheels.

PHOTO: Husqvarna riding mower.

PHOTO: *John Deere 4120 stuck in the mud.*

Chapter 10 — The Farm Name

We get many comments about our choice of the farm name, Perseverance Wild Blueberry Farm. "How did you come up with that name?" It is a rather convoluted path, but I will try to explain. Part of the blueberry process includes a controlled burn of the fields. This usually happens after the first frost. It is imperative that there is an adequate crew present with Indian Tanks. Because Perseverance Wild Blueberry farm is so remote and is some distance from a water supply it is a challenge to provide adequate water to fight any fire that may get out of control. Some years ago, I contemplated buying a pumper fire truck with a large water tank. At that time, I was working as the State Floodplain Management Coordinator at the State Planning Office. That job took me all over Maine doing community visits and assisting local Code Enforcement Officers.

On one of my trips, I was passing through Somerville, and I spotted a big red fire truck, a 1954 GMC 500 gallon pumper, for sale. I worked with another planner at the office who was a resident and chairman of the planning board in Somerville, and he put me in touch with the town's fire chief. I was encouraged to submit a bid, and so I did. A couple of weeks later I got a call from the fire chief: I was the winning bidder, and the new owner of the fire truck. I had a lot to learn about using the big midship pump and driving the beast. The truck was named The Judge by the fire department. Shortly after buying The Judge, Mardens, a large store that sells salvage and overstock items, had a big sale on fire equipment such as pikes, axes, and ancillary equipment. I bought some chrome items and in the

PHOTO: 1954 GMC General mid-ship pumper and 1952 Ford F7 front mount pumper. 2009.

book section I found a book about old fire houses, so I bought it too. The book was The Firehouse, by Rebecca Zurier, 1982. On page 41 was a photograph of a fireman with the Philadelphia Perseverance Fire Hose Company, circa 1871. That name, Perseverance, hit me. My in-laws wanted to call the farm Blueberry Ridge Farm Number 3. Nancy's parents owned Blueberry Ridge Farm in Sebec, and her sister and brother-in-law owned blueberry land in Barnard. The Blueberry Ridge Farm Number Three did not settle with me, so I showed the photo to Nancy and suggested we call the farm Perseverance. She liked it. Her mother appeared a bit disappointed but eventually accepted the new name.

A few years later I was doing another community visit in Mapleton, up in Aroostook County. They had a beautiful 1952 F7 Ford pumper fire truck with a front mount pump sitting out behind the town office. I told John Edgecomb, the Town Manager, I had a fire truck, and he quickly informed me that the Ford was not for sale. That was fine with me. I already had a fire truck. A few months later

John called me and reminded me of the beautiful Ford. "If you want it, talk to the fire chief and make an offer."

Long story short, I bought a second fire truck. Bringing this firetruck down to central Maine was an experience. A couple of friends offered to help me get it. John Del Vecchio and Don. We rode up to Mapleton in Don's car and John Edgecomb_was waiting for us at the town office. I gave John the check then took the truck to fill the gas tank. It was a brutal, cold, gray, January day. I stopped at Walmart in Presque Isle to buy a gas can for just in case the gas gauge wasn't accurate. The beautiful truck had some age on her, and she wasn't happy about driving down Interstate 95. She was used to doing short runs to local fires. There were holes in the floorboards where presumably previous equipment had been attached and the areas around the gas, brake and clutch pedals also allowed the cold air to flow into the cab. Don followed us in his car while John in the passenger seat was busy looking for rags or anything else he could use to stuff the holes and stop the infiltration of winter's breath. The heater worked, sort of. It never got that warm in the cab. We finally made it to Let and Nellie's house in Sebec where the truck would spend the rest of the winter until the weight limits were lifted on the local roads in Kingsbury. Nellie prepared a great meal for all of us. The guys were well fed and happy.

Chapter 11 — The Land

PHOTO: Wide stone wall that was the southern boundary of True Ames homestead, now part of the northern portion of Perseverance Wild Blueberry Farm.

As noted earlier, the farm is now 316 acres. The original purchase was 310 but later we added six and half acres adjacent to the west. The bulk of the farm, 241 acres lies north of Campbell Road, and 75 acres lie south of the road. The coordinates of the highest point of the farm, Cowett Hill, are N.45°07.163' and W.69°36.634'.

In 2011 we were the only easily accessible blueberry farm located in climatic Zone 4B according to a University of Maine graduate student engaged in dissertation research at our farm. The climate has changed through the years. According to the USDA Plant Hardiness zone maps for Maine, Kingsbury was in zone 4B (-25 degrees to -20 degrees Fahrenheit) in 1990, in zone 4A (-30 degrees to -25 degrees) in 2012, and in zone 5A (-20 degrees to -15 degrees) in 2023. Each zone is based on the 30-year average of the coldest temperature recorded each winter.

PHOTO: *This picture shows the width of the True Ames rock wall.*

The elevation of Cowett Hill is approximately 1,300 feet above sea level. The north slope of Cowett Hill drops in elevation to about 900 feet while still on the farm but continues to drop as the slope runs to Kingsbury Stream. The southern end of the farm, south of Campbell Road, is relatively flat with an average elevation of 1,000 feet.

There are a couple of wetland areas on the farm. The largest area is fed by a spring south of the orchard and there is a seasonal wet area just south of Campbell Road on the east end of the farm. It usually dries up in late summer. The fields are generally rocky as is typical of New England. Some fields were once cleared, but

PHOTO: *Generally, the larger rocks were placed on or near the bottom of the wall. This was all done before there were hydraulic loaders. It was all physical labor and the use of a stone boat to cart the rock to the wall with a team of horses or oxen.*

additional rocks have worked their way to the surface due to frost action. Many of the fields are either bordered by rock walls or traversed by massive rock walls. These walls were created generations ago when the farm was made up of small subsistence farms. The early settlers did the rock clearing by hand with the aid of horses. It is hard to imagine that some of the fields were at one time hay fields.

Soils are often classified by the relative proportions of sand, silt and clay particles as well as plasticity and organic matter content. Most of the soils on the north end of the farm are moderately sloping Chesuncook/Telos, which are moderately well drained. Along the western edge of the north end is a strip of gently sloping Telos/Monarda soils that are poorly drained. At the top of Cowett

Hill the soils are moderately sloping Monson/Elliotsville/Ricker, which are excessively well drained. Ricker series soils are shallow organic soils on mountains and hills. They form in thin organic deposits usually underlain by a thin mineral horizon over bedrock. The majority of the soils south of Campbell Road are moderately sloping Chesuncook/Elliotsville which are well drained. Chesuncook soils form in a deep glacial till and are generally forested. The eastern edge of the southern fields are moderately sloping Monson/Elliotsville/Ricker that are excessively well drained. The organic content of the soils means they are minimally impacted by drought except for ledges with thin soil. According to the Forest Management Plan for the farm in 1997, of the two hundred acres of wood there are eighty-six acres of hardwood, ninety-six acres of mixed wood and sixteen acres of birch and poplar.

PHOTO: Lou's attempt at rebuilding the rock wall along entrance lane to the farm.

PHOTO: *Lou's attempt at rebuilding the rock wall along entrance lane to the farm.*

Several years ago I decided to see how much I could do in rebuilding a rock wall without using any modern tools such as a tractor or excavator. I started with the west end of the wall along the entrance just beyond the elbow. I only got about 40 feet before the rocks grew too heavy and I gave up. What I did accomplish was leveling the top of the wall and making the sides more uniform.

Chapter 12 — The Harvest

Maine wild blueberry plants are one of the first plants in succession after the woods are cleared, usually by timber harvesting or fire. The blueberries are not planted annually. It takes decades if not centuries for a field to fully develop. The plants send out rhizomes (underground stems) that produce clones over time. The rhizomes only grow about an inch per year. By pruning the plants after the harvest, fertilizing the plants, and doing weed control, the fields gradually fill in. The wild blueberry plants like slightly acidic, well-drained soil. They prefer the sun and do not do well in shaded areas. Maine is ideal for blueberry plants. As the ice age progressed across Maine many centuries ago, the ice ground up a lot of granite which helps establish an ideal soil pH is between 4.0 and 4.8. The indigenous people found that burning the fields helped control the weeds and insects, a practice established by the settlers as well.

There are two types of wild low-bush blueberries: low sweets (*Vaccinium angustifolium*) and sour tops (*Vaccinium myrtilloides*). Low sweets have smooth leaves and stems. Blueberry color can range from light, powder blue to jet black. Sour tops primarily grow at higher elevations and on mountain tops. Its leaves and stems have fine, white hairs and the plants are usually more branched than the low sweets: the leaves are velvety. The so called cultured or high bush blueberries are generally much larger in diameter than the wild low-bush blueberries. Science has shown us that the antioxidants, flavonoids and vitamin C are in the skin of the blueberry. If you compare a cup of the larger, cultured blueberries to a cup of wild blueberries the wild blueberries have nearly twice the antioxidant content, more polyphenols and lower sugar content. However, cultured blueberries are grown in every state in the Union and are less expensive.

PHOTO: *A raker using a 40 point blueberry rake.*

For the sake of discussion, I will start the wild blueberry cycle with the harvest. The routine starts for most of the Downeast growers with a harvest in late July or early August. Raking does not begin until the entire field is blue. But before the actual raking begins it is common practice to determine if blueberry fruit flies (*Rhagoletis mendax Curran*) are enough of a problem to warrant spraying with an insecticide before harvesting. The sampling begins a couple of weeks prior to raking. Sampling usually involves putting yellow sticky fly traps around the fields and then counting the flies the next day on the sticky sheets. After spraying the field, reentry time is about four hours but about three days before fruit consumption. Applications of one to two weeks allows ample time before harvesting and there are generally rain showers during that time. The fruit flies enter a field from the edges of the field, and many growers will only spray the perimeter of the field if flies are determined to be a problem.

Up until the 1990's the growers would hire huge numbers of individuals to rake the ripe blueberries. Growers Downeast employ significant numbers of migrant help. There are temporary housing units along some of the fields. The rakers use either handheld rakes or rakes on long handles, but with either, the work is arduous. The common blueberry rakes look like a dustpan with tines (some call them points or teeth) sticking out of the front of the pan and the handle is on top of the inside of the pan. The rakes come in various widths typically ranging in five point increments from 20 to 80 tines or points although some custom made rakes go beyond 100 points. Such large rakes do not work in a field with sour top blueberries such as ours. Our plants are more bushy with more stems and leaves that tend to cause the larger rakes to get stuck in the plant. Sometimes the weakest part of the rake gives way or the handle breaks. Some say, "Just weld it back on." "Not so!" I say. The rakes are made of thin galvanized metal, and welding will melt the rake. Broken rakes need to be soldered. To find someone who can give a solid and smooth soldering job is extremely difficult today. When we bought the farm in 1987 it was easy to just buy new rakes. You could buy a new rake for about a dollar a point, so a 40 point rake would cost around $40. It was not too many years later that the cost went to $2 a point. At about the same time growers were experiencing a shortage of labor. Young kids no longer wanted to nor needed to rake blueberries. "That's hard work." "I can't do that." "I won't do that." This was a statewide problem. Parents would give the kids whatever they needed. They no longer had to earn money for school supplies or clothes.

It has been said, necessity is the mother of invention. Zane Emerson of Columbia Falls grew up in the blueberry industry. His father was Dell Emerson, University of Maine Blueberry Hill Farm Manager. Zane was painfully aware of the labor crisis facing the growers so he began experimenting with mechanical harvesters. He eventually patented a walk-behind mechanical harvester that proved to be an excellent machine. Nancy's parents were always ready to try new methods and new equipment. They bought one of the very first Maine Blueberry Equipment harvesters and we soon followed suit. It wasn't long before most of the growers were using the new machines, and they proved to be a life saver for the industry. The machines showed up every day for work and did not goof off. Consequently, there was a lesser need for new rakes. The principal rake manufacturer, the C.H. Drisco and Brother Tabbut Company from Columbia Falls, Maine, had been in business since 1882. Modern technology contributed to those businesses closing. There is now another company that makes blueberry rakes: The Hubbard Rake Company in Jonesport, ME. They have been in business since 1990, and their rakes are all aluminum. A 40 point rake sold for just under $80 as of 2024. They have a long list of the various rake sizes. I am sure their rakes are just as good as, if not better than the Tabbut rakes, but I love the older rakes. I guess it is all about what you get used to.

To use the new harvesters, it was necessary to remove all the rocks in the fields. So, consequently, most blueberry fields have since been cleared of rocks and leveled to allow machine harvesting. There is a separate chapter about rock removal later in this book.

If a field is to be hand raked, the owner of the blueberry fields usually lines the fields with string creating raking lanes. We try to set ours at roughly ten feet wide but if the berries are sparse in a part of the field we will widen the lane a few feet. Running lines is a task that is done early in the morning before the customers begin to show up at 7:00 A.M. That means the individual running the lines starts at 6:00 or at least before 7:00 and it is a wet run. Most mornings the plants are wet with dew. The strings are tied off at the beginning and end of each row. It is more comfortable to wear high top boots and warm socks. We run the lines in the early morning because if we run them in the evening they are usually broken or strewn all over the field due to nocturnal animals crossing the field. The deer and moose tear them up, but it can also be the result of bears seeking a good blueberry meal. When running the lines it is a good idea to look for wasp nests. If one is found it needs to be flagged with a large set back of flagging tape running around it. Whoever is running the lines does not want to be stung and neither do the rakers.

A couple of weeks before we open, which is now around the beginning of August, we provide updates on our website www.perseverancefarm.com which include the opening date and price per pound for raking and custom orders. We also post our hours. A day before we open we place Perseverance Wild Blueberry Farm signs with an arrow pointing south to Campbell Road at the intersection of State Route 16 and Hotel Drive down by Kingsbury Pond and a second sign is placed at the "Y" of Campbell Road and Wellington Road again pointing south up Campbell Road. Following Campbell Road up the hill to the intersection with Campbell Road and the Leavett/Cross Road. Another Perseverance Blueberry sign is placed pointing west on Campbell Road.

The last sign is placed at the intersection of Campbell Road and Preble Lane pointing north, up Preble Lane. This sign is a big white tent sign advertising Wild Blueberries and our hours. Near the barn we have a new blue metal oval sign with the Perseverance Wild Blueberry Farm name on it. We also try to run ads in the local weekly newspapers. When customers drive to the farm we have a sign at the 'elbow' asking them to first check in at the barn before parking. I now have a stop sign at the south end of the barn. Many customers think the area near the winnowing tent is for customer parking, which it is not. That area is reserved for customers that have brought their berries down to be winnowed. If they are going to pick-their-own, I need to determine how many rakes and buckets I need to load in the back of the Kubota before picking them up to take them to the field.

PHOTO: the Rake Wall in the barn.

91

PHOTO: A customers homemade rake.

I have started preloading the Kubota with rakes and buckets in the morning before customers arrive in an effort to save some time. After determining their wishes as to picking up already processed berries or to pick-their-own, they are either told to park their vehicle behind the old house or to pull up to the barn to load.

I pick up the customers near their vehicles with the Kubota RTV and take them to a field that needs to be raked. An important set of questions we ask is, "Have you been here before? Have you raked before?" Many have no idea how to rake, so before they are given a rake they are given a brief lesson on how to use it. Of course, there are a few individuals who have raked blueberries for years and some

PHOTO: A customers homemade rake.

not only have their own rakes but have special handmade rakes. Some of the handmade ones are beautifully done.

I give new customers a fun quiz—naming the various parts of the rake. We try to have a good time with the quiz. We start with the tines, then the pan and the bottom fold or acute angle at the base of the pan, which we call the heel. Next, I try to teach them how to rake by running the tines under the berries and gently tipping the rake back and allowing the berries to roll into the back of the pan. "Rake gently and do not ram the rake full throttle into the plant." On occasion the rake may get caught on a stem gall in the crotch of the plant. "Do NOT try to pull the rake over or past the gall," I tell them. "I guarantee that they will break the rake. The handle will give way.

When or if you get to an issue where the rake won't move forward, back the rake out of the plant."

The galls are kidney-shaped or spherical growths that are half an inch to one and half inches in diameter on the blueberry stems. They are as hard as a rock. These growths are formed by midges or gall wasps which are quite tiny. The galls house many of insect larvae.

PHOTO: Blueberry galls compared to wild blueberries.

You don't need to break the gall off, just leave it. In years past when Mr. Preble owned the farm, I am told he would pay the young rakers a penny apiece for the galls if they would break them off and turn them in when they brought their blueberries to the winnowing station. If you look closely at the galls you may see some tiny holes and those holes are caused by insects making their way out of the gall. This is usually only seen when the gall has turned brown with age, late in the season.

After raking the berries from the upper part of the plant I show them that there are often a lot of berries under the canopy. Customers are generally amazed at how easy it looks. I then ask how they get the berries from the rake pan into the five gallon pail. Most think it is to tip the rake forward and let the berries roll out across the tines. "NOooo!" I explain that the problem with doing it that way is that the rake is wider than the bucket and the berries follow the space between the tines and a lot of berries roll to the ground. The best way to get the berries into the bucket is to pour the berries from a back corner of the rake.

Power raking is not allowed. To which I'm frequently asked, "What is power raking?" I demonstrate by wielding the rake at a fast pace and ramming the tines into the plant rapidly several times and pulling the rake out roughly. Sometimes I may end up pulling a plant out of the ground. The usual response is "Oh No!.. We won't do that." I explain that if they rake like that, they end up with blue soup and they rapidly wear themselves out. More importantly, my rakes, which are almost as old as I am, break and I cannot replace them. The handle is the weakest part of the rake and continued stress on it will cause it to break. It is nearly impossible to find anyone who can solder a strong joint, so I ask customers to treat the rakes with respect. "If you break it… I cry." Before I leave customers to rake on their own I have them demonstrate for me how to rake and put the berries into the pail. I then wish them happy raking. I explain that we ask that they rake clean, in other words rake all the berries in the row and not jump around for just the good looking spots. After they finish a row (if they last that long) and if they still want more, they should take the next available row. There are no jumping rows just because you may think a row further down the field looks better. We need to have the entire field raked. It's been said you cannot have mountains without valleys. We need to rake the good with the bad.

If families have youngsters, I ask that the children not run through the fields. While I know it may be fun running through the fields, it knocks the berries off the plants and makes raking difficult for the next customers. Additionally, there are rocks to trip over and in some places there are raspberry and blackberry bushes with thorns. I also advise that children under the age of ten should not use a rake for fear that someone might get stabbed with the sharp points. In fact, misuse of the rakes can cause the rakes to break. Furthermore, children often get bored with raking and put the rake down and forget where they put it. I hate it when I run over a rake with the flail mower in the fall. With all that being said, I do expect the kids to come down to the winnowing tent with blue lips, teeth and tongues. We do not charge extra for the eaten blueberries.

Before getting back in the buggy, I ask the customers if they have any last minute questions and if they have a cell phone. If they have cell phones, I give them my cell phone number so they can call me to pick them up when they are done and they do not have to lug their bucket(s) of berries down to the winnowing tent. Unfortunately, not everyone has good cell reception and therefore they cannot call me. Before leaving I watch them as I turn the buggy around and most of them are pouring from the front of the tines. I stop, and in good fun, I give them a refresher course. My tutorials are frequently interrupted by my cell phone. Nancy often calls to inform me I have more customers waiting to be picked up. This routine continues until closing time, which on weekdays is until 12 P.M. and on the weekends it is 3 P.M. As the customers finish raking and I pick them up or they walk back to the winnowing tent, I prepare them for the next step in the harvest: Winnowing.

Chapter 13 — Winnowing

Eons ago winnowing was a primitive process. Indigenous people all over the world relied on natural wind to remove the leaves, dirt and chaff from their harvested product, which was usually seeds or nuts. The seeds or nuts would be thrown up in the air, and the wind would blow out the chaff. The seeds would land on the sieve screens held by the individual.

PHOTO: Emil Rivers plate on machine.

In the early 1900's, primitive technology was beginning to evolve. Early winnowing machines were hand cranked. Two guys would do the winnowing. One guy would pour the berries into the hopper while the second would turn the crank. Turning the crank fast enough to generate enough wind to blow out the leaves was hard work and about every fifteen minutes the two guys would switch places to give their arms a rest. I have seen pictures of an older model of Emil River's machine that was hand cranked with the largest pulley on the far end of the machine having the crank handle. In 1926 Emil Rivers patented a blueberry winnower, and he went into production in 1932. At about that time Briggs and Stratton (B&S) was creating their small single-cylinder gas engines. The B&S engines were being employed on a lot of various pieces of equipment, including the blueberry winnowing machines. Most of Emil River's machines were equipped with B&S engines. The earlier machines had cast iron engines, but the later models had aluminum ones.

PHOTO: Winnowing machines lined up in the tent with tables.

We have a large 12′ x 20′ tent dedicated to winnowing. The tent is erected below the orchard on a reasonably level area. A_tarp to catch the leaves and material blown out from the winnowing machines is put down next to the tent.. The tarp is cleaned nightly.

PHOTO: Winnowing machine with gas engine.

Next we lay down four three by six foot rubber stall mats with about four feet between each. The mats provide an area for the customers to stand and avoid any mud if it rains. The mats also make cleaning up easier each night. After the mats are laid, the old antique winnowing machines are set in place. As part of the set up the machines have to be cleaned, leveled and greased. During the harvest season it is advisable to grease the machines periodically. I have put blue plastic lids over the exposed shaft ends to help keep the customers from getting grease on themselves while winnowing. The generators are placed between the winnowing machines and filled with gas. This is done daily.

The original Briggs and Stratton engines were a huge improvement over the hand crank system, but they were noisy and required a lot of maintenance including oil changes, cleaning or

PHOTO: Danger sign.

PHOTO: Winnowing machine with electric motor.

adjusting the carburetor, and changing the spark plug. It was also impossible to carry on a conversation with the machine running. It belched out a foul smelling exhaust and required frequent servicing of the gas tank. The small tank had to be filled several times a day. It was not a good mix to have the person pouring blueberries onto the machine after getting gasoline on his/her hands. In 2005 we converted four of our Emil Rivers machines to use electric motors. We can now run two winnowing machines all day on one tank of gas with the efficient Honda 2000 generator. The Hondas are quiet and run smoothly. Our little Hondas are now over twenty years old and are still performing well. Maintenance is key to keeping the machines in good working order. We have two Honda 2000s running four winnowers.

Before I show the customers how to winnow I advise them to pour half the blueberries into another five gallon bucket. I show the customer the proper way to set the bucket on the machine, and how to pour the berries onto the short top conveyor belt. It is important to roll the berries around on the belt to ensure that clumps are broken up. If they are not broken up, the wind from the winnowing fan will catch them and carry them to the waste pile. A second person in the customer's group sits at the end of the machine where the berries roll out into the collection pan. If they see anything that falls into the pan that they do not want to eat, they pick it out and throw it into the trash flat next to where they are seated rather than throw it onto the ground.

While I explain how well the machine works and what a wonderful job it can do for them, it is not without risk. Many years ago a lady was pouring her berries from the belt side of the machine which is a no-no. She got part of her anatomy caught in the belts. The belts went flying off the pulleys and she was not only embarrassed but bruised. We now have a sign on that side of each of the machines telling customers "DANGER DO <u>NOT</u> STAND ON THIS SIDE OF THE MACHINE." I also ask the parents to ensure that their children stay away from the belt side of the machines.

Several years ago Nancy was working alone. After everyone had left for the day. I had gone back to work in Augusta because my working vacation was over. Nancy had long blond hair worn in pigtails at the time. As she bent over to check the berries in the receiving pan under the machines, her hair got sucked in around the paddle fan shaft. She grabbed the remaining hair in both hands to save her scalp while trying to reach the shut-off switch on the other end of the machine with her foot. Impossible! There she was, bent over with her hair caught around the shaft in Kingsbury which had a population of three. At that time the nearest neighbor would not hear her screams, so she didn't bother. After several minutes the electric motor overheated and shut off from the stress, but the ends of her hair were still wrapped around the greasy fan shaft.

As luck would have it, one of our early morning customers, George Scott, happened to be out driving around with his daughter. He drove up to the barn to check things out and that is when he saw Nancy and her need for help. He rescued her hair, but the electric motor wouldn't start again until the next day. While I tell these stories to all my new customers, several years ago it happened again. We had a large church group in the winnowing tent, and I gave my usual admonitions before turning them loose to winnow. There was a young lady about to start her freshman year of high school. She did the same thing Nancy had done. This time she not only got caught, the machine ripped out her hair. It was a traumatic experience for everyone. Several members of the group told me it was not my fault because I had warned them before of the potential risks. Just the same, I felt terrible. The young lady got a lot of attention, and unfortunately I never heard any more about her until a year later. She was okay. I had replaced some of the screens around the intakes for the paddle fans, but there will always be an element of risk. I try to remind customers that it is important to be respectful of the machine.

While the customers are winnowing I try to engage them in a friendly conversation. I like to know where they are from and what their occupation is. I usually tell a joke or story. Most customers enjoy a good joke and the friendly atmosphere. Over the years I have made a lot of friends and have come to look forward to seeing them again a year later. It is not uncommon to have someone come up to me at the grocery store and say "Hi, how are the blueberries looking for this year." It sometimes takes me a few minutes to realize who they are, but we usually end up in a good conversation.

When the customers come down to the winnowing tent with their five gallon buckets of blueberries, they are greeted with a clean environment or at least we try to keep it clean. Following the Covid epidemic of 2019 and 2020 we needed to rethink how we handled the customers and their products. We hung plastic shower curtains between each of the winnowing stations and bought clear plastic liners for the pans used to capture the berries after they came out of the winnowing machine. We placed bottles of Purell hand sanitizer on the tables and had masks available for anyone who wanted one.

At the end of my winnowing lesson, I told the customers that one way we tried to keep the cost down for the pick-your-own is we asked them to help keep the place clean. They are provided with clean buckets, and rakes, when they come to the farm and are provided with a clean machine to winnow. We want them to clean the buckets, rakes, pans and the machine when they are finished. When finished winnowing, it is important to remove the fresh blueberries in the pan under the machine before cleaning the machine. The berries are put on a big table provided near the winnower. If a customer puts their berries on the ground my dog might eat them — she loves blueberries. We provide blue microfiber towels and a five gallon bucket with a bit of bleach in the water for cleaning the machine. I ask our customers to wring out the excess water from the towel over the water bucket. Otherwise, as the day progresses we end up with a muddy mess around the bucket which can become a slip and fall hazard.

I show them how to fold the blue towels to wipe down the machine. While the towel should be wrung out it should be wet enough to clean. The top belt gets wiped down first and the best way to do so is to hold the wet towel against the edge of the belt as the machine is running. When the belt has made a full revolution the towel is refolded to provide a clean part of the towel before moving it over to clean the next portion of the belt. This is done until the belt is clean. Afterwards we rinse out the towel and proceed to wipe down the bigger conveyor belt following the same procedure. After the big belt is cleaned the machine must be turned off at the switch on the left leg of the machine. Again, rinse out the towel and wipe out the chute in the area where the berries fall into the pan. The waste flat should be put under the chute to catch the debris. We also have a five gallon bucket with a lid that serves as a waste bucket for paper towels and used plastic liners.

Chapter 14 — The Barn Set Up

In 2013 we radically changed the way we process the blueberries for customers that don't want to pick their own. We now have equipment that allows us to process more orders and do it in a cleaner, more efficient manner. Each employee is provided an apron and access to blue microfiber towels. There are six separate pieces that make up the total pick over equipment: the platform, the feed conveyor, the winnower, the string table, the slant table and the 10 foot pick-over conveyor. Each of these pieces is important to the quality of the end product, a flat of beautiful healthy blueberries. In preparation for the annual blueberry processing in the barn, the six

PHOTO: Feed conveyor.

PHOTO: The platform.

pieces of the processing equipment are cleaned and prepped for the run. I will try to explain the relevance of each part of the system.

PHOTO: Waste side of string table.

The first piece is the platform with its access steps. This is where the person stands to pour and spread the blueberries on to the feed conveyor. The platform has no moving parts, so it is cleaned and sometimes painted before each harvest season. However, the person

PHOTO: *Sheet covering giant winnowing module with the squirrel cage blower in the base.*

on the platform has control over the speed of the feed conveyor and the switch for the big winnower.

The second piece is the feed conveyor. This is where an employee pours and spreads the berries onto the conveyor belt as they are moved to the giant winnower. Prior to opening day, it is cleaned and the "zipper" for the conveyor belt is checked to ensure that the wire that holds the zipper together is not working its way out of the ends and scoring the insides of the frame, which it has a habit of doing. When it does it makes a horrendous screeching noise and demands immediate attention. It mandates a shutdown until it is repaired.

The big winnower with a squirrel cage fan is the third piece. It is cleaned after sitting all winter. When it is running the debris falls into a large garbage can on wheels on the exhaust air side of the machine. A waste can is placed under the exit chute and must be emptied every few hours. Not all the leaf debris flows out the exhaust chute

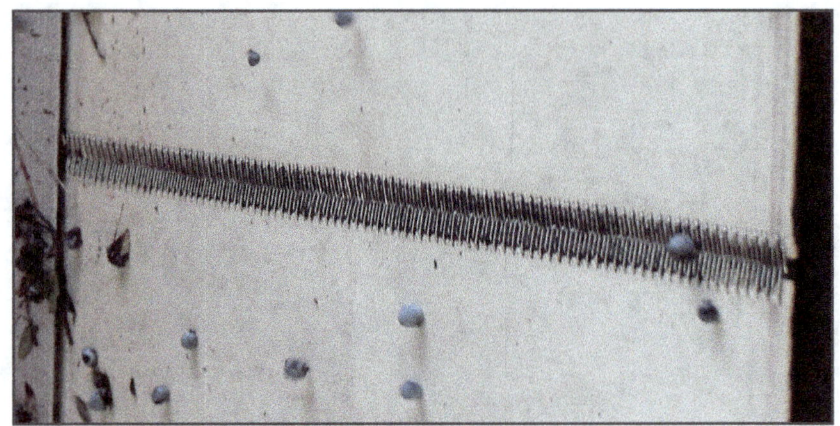

PHOTO: *Conveyer zipper.*

and over the course of the season a lot of the leaves tumble down to the bottom of the squirrel cage housing. The machine must be partially disassembled, and a vacuum cleaner is used to clean it out. The chute on the far side of the winnower, where the blueberries come out often clogs due to berries with stems or in clumps get caught in the perforations in the chute. This has to be cleaned daily and requires some partial disassembly. The berries exiting the winnower fall onto the string table, the fourth piece in the processing line up.

The string table is a challenge to describe. It is made up of three rollers and sixty plastic chords (strings) that rotate over the rollers. The rollers form an upside-down triangle with the top side running horizontal. The strings run perpendicular to the rollers, and each of the sixty strings is set in a groove on each roller. The spacing of the strings allows the tiny berries to fall through the spaces between the strings into a trough that sends them to trash bins. The larger berries follow the strings as they rotate and drop onto the slant table as discussed next. During setup its position is checked so the strings

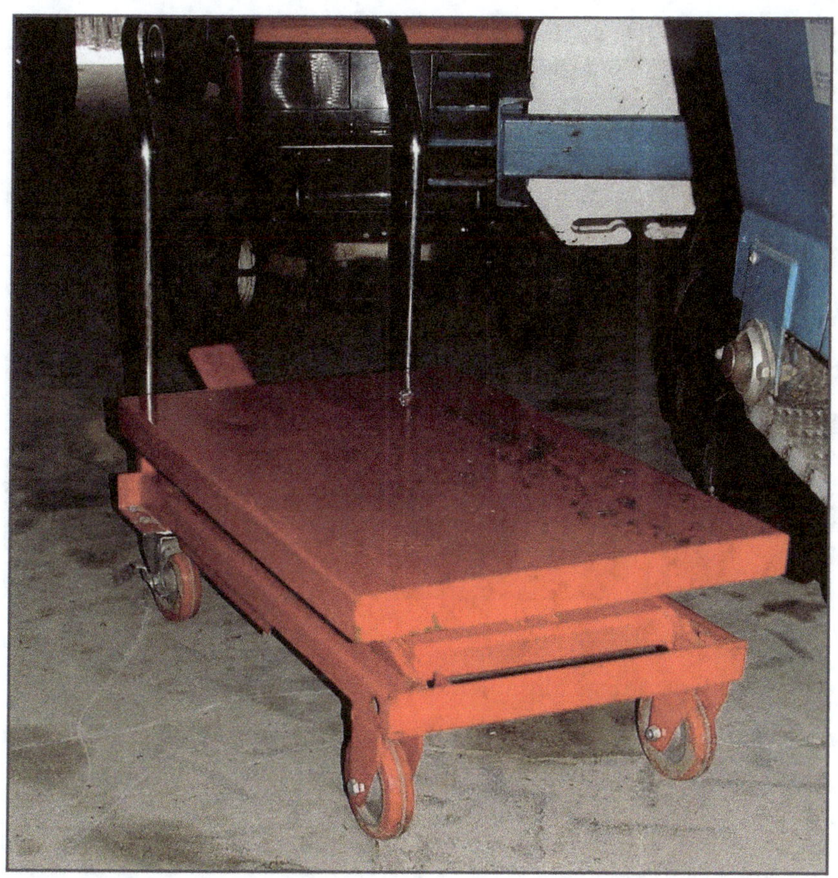

PHOTO: *Low wheeled cart at end of long conveyer.*

are not rubbing the outlet side of the winnower. At the end of the day the string table needs to be cleaned. The strings get sticky and dirty as well as the rollers. To put it mildly, it is a real pain to clean and very time consuming. No one wants that job. Some make a halfhearted attempt, but no one cleans it as well as I do and it usually falls back on me to clean up after it is "cleaned." Being off the grid and without running water makes it all the more difficult to clean it. I would love to see some sort of high pressure water supply to loosen the crud, but then I would need a floor drain.

PHOTO: Slant table.

The slant table alignment is a short conveyor that runs perpendicular to the flow of the berries. It is tilted at a slight angle and is positioned between the string table and the ten foot conveyor. The sticky or squished berries, as well as clumps of berries, go off the end of the slant table into waste containers, too.

The ten foot conveyor table is where a big part of the pick over action occurs. It has positions for three people on one side and two on the other. Stools are provided for those who wish to sit as they pick. As the berries roll from the slant table onto the long conveyor it provides the staff the opportunity to closely look over the berries and remove any imperfect berries or any other items that are not blueberries such as seeds, sticks and leaves that survived the winnower and string table. There are waste containers stationed around both sides of the long conveyor for disposing of the unwanted items. There is a rheostat on the side of the conveyor to

PHOTO: *Ten foot conveyer where berries get final pick over - 4 people are working the table.*

adjust the speed on the belt. If there is a high volume of berries hitting the table it is sometimes necessary to slow the belt down to give the staff time to examine all the berries. By the time the berries get to the end of the belt they are very clean as they drop into the appropriate containers for the orders. The boxes are lined up on a low wheeled cart which gets moved back and forth periodically as the boxes get filled. Lorry, who has been with us for many years, is excellent at switching out the containers as they fill and replacing them with empty containers without incident. The bulk of our orders are completed in ten pounds of berries per box. The receiving boxes are usually cardboard flats that are ideal. Lorry takes each flat to the scale that is already tared for the flats and ensures the weight is ten pounds. She labels the flat with the last name of the customer and puts it in the baker's racks along the side of the work area. During slack times or before the machines are started in the morning, or after lunch, the boxes are assembled and stacked for the next group of orders to be filled. The crew starts at 6:00 AM. They break at 9:00 AM

PHOTO: Rheostat to control the speed on each machine.

and again for lunch at noon. Each morning, before turning on the various machines, Robert fills the Honda 300 generator with gas, just outside of the barn. The five electric motors that drive the various modules are plugged in and turned on in the proper sequence. The feed conveyor is first, the big winnowing fan which pulls the most

PHOTO: Rolling scaffolding loaded with blueberries.

power is second. Next, the string table, the slant table, and lastly the ten foot conveyor. There is also a rheostat on each machine allowing a separate speed adjustment for each.

The berries that are brought in from the field are stacked on the platform leaving enough room for the person pouring the berries on the feed conveyor to do his/her job. Up to 24 flats may be stacked on the platform. More berries are loaded onto a rolling portable scaffold that can hold an additional 14 flats. If additional berries are brought in and more space is needed, they are stacked on the barn floor on top of a few upside down plastic flats beyond the platform and rolling scaffold. They are kept near the platform within easy reach. The person putting berries on the feeding conveyor is responsible for adjusting the speed on the belt and spreading the berries uniformly across the belt. If there are too many berries at a time the machine will not winnow the leaves or other trash as well. Once the box being dumped on the belt is empty, it is brushed out with a small whisk broom, and the box is stacked on a table next to the belt assembly. Those flats will be thoroughly washed later. The individual doing the feed conveyor is also responsible for keeping an eye on the trash receptacles at the big winnower, the string table and slant table. When the trash bins get full, they are emptied into the larger trash can and taken to the winnowing waste pile outside the barn. The floor is swept with a corn broom and then mopped. The floor gets slick with smashed blueberries, and it is worse under and around the string table, slant table and ten foot conveyor belt. Even with strategically placed waste receptacles the berries do not always fall where we think they should. The wastewater is dumped in the orchard, and the organic waste feeds the fruit trees. The dirty

PHOTO: Emil Rivers Winnowing machine painted Royal Blue.

microfiber towels are collected, put in a container and taken back to Guilford to be washed.

In the winnowing tent there are small signs taped to the two four by eight foot tables reminding the customers to clean out their rakes, winnowing machine when done, and clean out their five gallon pails. The winnowing tent also gets a thorough cleaning every evening

PHOTO: 1969 John Deere 1020 repainted in 2021.

PHOTO: Cedar picnic table stained in Cottonwood Gray and Yellow, 2024.

after all the pick-your-own customers have left. The area around the winnowing machines is cleaned with a broom and the large tarp where the winnowing machine debris collects is swept into a big pile and loaded into a large trash can that is emptied onto the winnowing pile behind the barn. The winnowing debris pile eventually becomes good compost material for gardens and the orchard. The winnowing machines get a shot of grease in each of the six grease fittings at the various shafts that support the belts. The scales, calculator, note pad, towels and rakes are collected and secured in the barn for the night. The water bucket for washing the winnowing machine belts is emptied in the orchard and refilled with clean bleach water. The five gallon waste bucket is checked and if needed, emptied into the larger waste can in the barn.

At the end of the season there are tons of plastic boxes to clean. We bought a stainless steel milk parlor sink for part of that process and it is placed under the solar panels at the mobile home site. The cleanup is done at the mobile home site where we have a good supply of water from the drilled well and can use the power washer if needed. Each container is washed, rinsed and put on the Kubota to be taken back to the barn and stored for the next season.

During the summer leading up to the harvest, after cleaning the equipment it is often necessary to repaint some of them. The John Deere 1020 got that treatment in the summer of 2021, and the antique winnowing machines got repainted with royal blue while the big pulleys were painted silver in 2023. We try to keep a supply of various spray cans of paint that match the original colors of the equipment; John Deere green, yellow, and black; Kubota orange; and Caterpillar yellow and black. Royal Blue is also on hand to touch up the winnowing machines. The new picnic table was stained with two different pastel stains, cottonwood gray and cottonwood yellow, in the summer of 2024. In 2023 the various tables and benches were repaired and re-stained in cottonwood gray.

The barn was built in 1993 and finished in September of that year. We had it stained in Cottonwood gray. In 2010 we hired Joel

White to repaint it. In 2019, I began repainting the barn again starting with the east wall and I have continued, as time allows, getting as far as finishing the north wall in 2024. While a step ladder works fine for doing the sidewalls, an extension ladder is necessary for painting the gable ends. It requires a lot of scraping and resetting a lot of the nails in the shiplap siding. Thirty years takes a toll on buildings.

PHOTO: Worktable.

PHOTO: Picnic Table with tent.

PHOTO: Pedestrian door sill had rotted and demanded repair.

PHOTO: West wall of barn being repainted in 2010.

PHOTO: Gallons of various weights of oil for different equipment.

PHOTO: A pin on the 3-point hitch gave way allowing the five foot flail mower to come loose from one side of the tractor.

PHOTO: I save every nut, bolt, pin, washer, screw and small part I can get my hands on.

Chapter 15 — Equipment Wear & Tear

There is no question that farming is hard on the equipment. The tractors and other equipment all demand a certain amount of maintenance. Oil and filter changes are necessary every so many hours of use plus greasing the various fittings daily, when used. Leaks need to be fixed before failure occurs. Tires wear out and hydraulics need servicing. The daily ritual is to check the crankcase oil, the hydraulic fluid as well as the antifreeze levels before starting the tractor engine. It is important to keep track of which piece of equipment has been serviced and when it should be serviced next time.

It is imperative to keep a supply of needed filters and quantities of various oil weights in stock. Different pieces of equipment demand differing weights of oil. Equipment without oil filters usually takes 30 weight, and the tractors take 10w30, and we prefer to use a synthetic oil. We also keep 90w gear oil, hydraulic oil by the five gallon can, chain and bar oil, and at least a gallon of antifreeze. We keep WD40, Loctite, Marvel Mystery oil, hydraulic jack oil, several tubes of grease, and brake fluid, on the shelves. Due to constant vibration of some equipment, it is wise to check the nuts and bolts as they can loosen or completely let go. There is a frequent need for various nuts, bolts and hitch pins as well. Belts can stretch and eventually break. We also have several clearing saws, and chain saws that require synthetic two cycle oil.

Owning a farm is an excuse to buy adult toys—tools and more tools. Eventually each piece of equipment has its own toolbox with dedicated tools specifically for that machine. The machines that have tires on them require an air compressor, which requires a generator, to keep the air pressure at the proper inflation so the equipment rolls easily. One thing leads to another. We have six generators, each with a dedicated use. Five of the generators are Hondas and one is an 8000 watt Onan, which powers the Lincoln Welder. The two Honda 2000s are for powering the winnowing machines in the winnowing tent. The Honda 3000 powers the five electric motors on processing machines as well as the three rows of overhead lights and fan, and there is a liquid cooled Honda 5000 for general purposes. It is the first generator and oldest of our generators and we bought it used in 1993. The Honda LP 6500 powers the mobile home when the solar panels cannot keep up with the demand. The walk behind harvester is a very complex machine with a system of chains and gears that baffles the mind as to how it works. Its rugged construction is imperative to its success, but there are times when a chain link may break or another component comes loose due to the thick vegetation and uneven ground. It requires constant monitoring to ensure all the pieces are tightened and in proper working order. It is a huge problem if it breaks down. It is, in essence, the heart of the harvest. The bottom line is preventative maintenance and vigilance are the key to keeping the harvester functioning. Robert is the key to taking care of the machine.

PHOTO: Honda 500 generator.

PHOTO: Drive belt on Befco flail mower is about to break.

Chapter 16 — Customers

A few people from Skowhegan and Cambridge, who sold produce at roadside stands, asked if we would sell blueberries to them wholesale so they could sell them at their stands. This was the beginning of our customer base. We enjoyed a remarkable friendship with those hard working individuals who would show up almost every morning by 7:00 AM to get their berries. At first some of them would rake their own, but as time passed and we became more efficient in processing the berries for customers, they began placing next day orders for 40 to 100 lbs. of berries. At one point we had five roadside stand customers. As time passed some of them retired and sadly a couple of them passed away.

There is one customer who stands out: George Scott from Cambridge, Maine. He was our most loyal customer, visiting us every morning with his daughter, Kathy. George and I had a lot in common. We both worked for state government, although different states, and we shared a lot of jokes. We sometimes would perform a fake argument in front of other customers and threaten to "take it outside," then engage in a hearty laugh. Some of his customers would place significant orders through him. After George died I calculated that he was about 17% of our annual business. Sadly, we no longer have daily resale individuals buying a large supply of blueberries. There is a roadside blueberry void in the region. While we certainly miss his large orders, we really miss them, especially George and his daughter.

Families are another big part of our customer base. Parents bring their children for a morning of blueberry picking. Kids are taken aback when I talk like Donald Duck. I try to entertain the older kids with silly jokes, and I have a litany of elephant jokes that were popular in the 1960's. For the adults, when there are no kids around, I have a supply of adult jokes. Of course, I make sure they would like to hear that kind of story before telling one. Our customers often tell me new jokes that I add to my repertoire.

Senior citizens are an increasing number of our customers, and most of them are from the Greenville area with some from Dover-Foxcroft. Of course, many more are from all over the region surrounding Kingsbury Plantation.

We have made so many friends over the past four decades that I would love to list them all but I know we would inadvertently forget someone and then feel bad. We love them all.

PHOTO: George Scott.

PHOTO: Maine Blueberry Equipment walk behind harvester

PHOTO: Befco five foot flail mower.

PHOTO: Nancy with the Troy-bilt sickle bar mower.

130

PHOTO: Nancy with the Kinco sickle bar mower.

PHOTO: Let on the 460 4-wheel drive Long Tractor.

Chapter 17 — Building the Business

Getting to where we are today was a slow process: building the structures, building our equipment inventory to manage the farm and more importantly, building the customer base. By reasonable measures, Perseverance Wild Blueberry Farm should not exist where it is. The farm is distant from local markets and labor. However, we have persevered with the good graces of loyal customers and hard work with little pay. The first couple of years, we relied solely on selling to the freezer plant. As the folks that I worked with learned I had a blueberry farm they started requesting that I sell blueberries directly to them. So, I did. At the same time, we were experiencing significant challenges hiring rakers. As noted earlier, the new generation of young people found it was easier to ask their parents for what they needed and therefore did not need to earn the money for school supplies. The older generation got older, and many found they could no longer tolerate the back breaking stress of raking. So, we are forced to rely on mechanical harvesting.

In 1992 Let and Nellie gave us a Kinco sickle bar mower to mow the rough fields. That mower was one of the best. It was rugged construction and rarely needed repairs. I tried to order a new one but found out that the company was bought out on the same day I tried to place my order. The lady on the phone was in tears. They were bought by Troy-Bilt. Although they had the machine I wanted in stock they were not allowed to sell it. We eventually bought a Troy-Bilt in 2000, but it did not last. The sickle bar frequently broke.

PHOTO: Box winnower.

In 1994, Let loaned us two tractors. The first was a 1969, 40 horsepower, 1020 John Deere with a 475 Kelly Loader. It included two sets of draw bars, a three foot bucket and an eight foot snow bucket. The second was a 45 horsepower, 1970 four-wheel drive, diesel, Long 460, made in Romania, which included two drawbars and a set of Canadian chains for the rear tires.

As the years passed we came to the realization we needed even more equipment In the same year we got the tractors we purchased two box winnowers. At that time, we did the winnowing in the field, and these were easy to move as needed. One person could easily lift one in and out of the back of a pickup. We also acquired a 36 inch Rhino Flail Mower with an eight horsepower Briggs & Stratton

PHOTO: Hobart wire feed welder.

Engine that can be pulled behind a riding lawn mower or a four wheeler.

Soon after that purchase we bought a used five foot Befco flail mower from Whittemore and Sons in Skowhegan. It has numerous knives that hang on a rotating drum and is PTO powered. In 1998 we purchased a second used five foot Befco flail mower. The big spacious barn began to fill up.

1996 was also a busy equipment acquisition year. Nancy bought a chisel plow to assist in rock removal. She also bought a Cyclone fertilizer spreader, which is used not only for fertilizer but also for herbicide. We also had a platform built with a three point hitch so we could move equipment with a tractor.

Another gain was from Maine Blueberry Equipment Company: a 50 gallon Automatic Mist Blower - Model MB50H, powered by the

PTO shaft. It was about this time that I bought the first firetruck as noted earlier. A neighbor, Ray Leavett, allowed me to park the firetruck on his property until the spring thaw when it would be safe

PHOTO: Honda Foreman 4X4.

PHOTO: 2005 John Deere 4120 with loader and flail mower.

to take it up Preble Lane to our barn. I bought a huge green tarp at Mardens to protect the firetruck until then.

PHOTO: Chisel plow.

In 1997, another busy year for filling the barn, we bought a new Roll Over Protection system (ROPS) for the JD 1020. Onie Lougie installed it for us. Onie also custom built a three point hitch water tank with a Homelight pump and hose reel for us to use when we burned the fields.

To facilitate serious repairs involving broken metal, I bought a portable Hobart wire feed welder followed by a Lincoln/Electric Ranger 8, Arc Welder with an Onan 8,000 watt AC power generator.

In 2000, we bought an experimental harvester out of Prince Edward Island (PEI), Canada, which we had mounted on the Long Tractor. We had to sell the tractor to the manufacturer in PEI to be custom fitted with the big harvester. In the middle of all of this, Nancy was deployed to Puerto Rico because of Hurricane Hugo. At that time, she was a FEMA Disaster Assistant Employee (DAE). She made all the arrangements to get the tractor to Canada, but I had no

PHOTO: Lou on Long Tractor with Cyclone spreader attached.

clue how or what to do to get it back to the US. Some of the paperwork got lost and the tractor, with its new harvester, sat at the Mane/Canadian Border. I had no fax machine to send the needed

PHOTO: Automatic, 50 gallon mist sprayer.

documentation, but our friend Marie Lougee stepped in to help, and
we got the machine back to Kingsbury. The manufacturer made
several trips to the farm over the next couple of weeks to tweak
adjustments. During the first year of operation, Nancy hit a rock and
the impact ripped the bolts holding the harvester from the tractor's
belly pan. Weak metal.

PHOTO: Befco five foot flail mower.

PHOTO: My daughter, Silisha moving the 2002 Caterpillar mini excavator 301.6 with a thumb.

PHOTO: Water tank with hose reel minus the Homelite pump.

PHOTO: Nancy, Lorry and Morley our Scottie with a load of empty boxes on the Kubota 1140.

PHOTO: Lincoln/Electric Ranger 8, arc welder with an 8,000 watt Onan generator.

PHOTO: 1952 Ford 8N tractor.

PHOTO: Nancy on the Long 460 tractor hitched to the Canadian blueberry harvester Circa 2003.

When I was a kid my family would visit my Uncle Jim, in southwest Missouri. I remember his Ford 8N tractor fondly and having a farm I got the idea that I, too, should have an 8N. In 2001 I saw one for sale on Rt. 150 as we were driving to the farm from Oakland. We stopped and bought it. It had been named Esmeralda.

PHOTO: 2005 Grapple bucket for 4120.

My plan was to use it as a water source when burning the fields, and it worked out well. It was able to travel the rough terrain of the rocky fields better than a heavy firetruck.

When my mother died in 2002, my uncle came to the funeral and I told him that I bought a Ford 8N just like the one he had. It turns out that he had a 9N. I sold the 8N in 2008 as I was in the process of converting it from a 6 volt system to 12 volt.

PHOTO: 800 cc Polaris Sportsman 4x4.

In 2004 we bought our first four wheeler, a yellow Honda Foreman Hondamatic from a dealer in Newport. However, in 2010 the transmission went bad, so in 2011 it was replaced with a 500 cc, Polaris Sportsman with a winch and cargo box.

Our biggest equipment acquisition was in 2005 when we bought a new four wheel drive John Deere 4120 three cylinder diesel tractor with a loader, 43-horsepower, and Power-Reverser at Hammond Tractor in Fairfield. We had the dealer install hydraulic lines to the rear of the tractor. In 2009 we purchased a Frontier 66" Grapple bucket from Hammond Tractor which is used not only for rock clearing, but also for picking up brush piles.

I bought a mini excavator as Nancy's Christmas present in 2006. It's a Caterpillar 301.6 with a thumb. It was bought to provide a better tool for rock removal, and the thumb facilitates easier removal

PHOTO: Bruce Grant testing the Hardi Boom Sprayer.

of the rock from its hole. I am pleased that it is a Caterpillar because my dad worked for Cat for 39 years at its East Peoria, IL facility.

I use the mini excavator to dig the big rocks out of the ground. I then push them to the edge of the field. I consider the mini Caterpillar to be the best adult toy ever.

We bought a new 2010 Kubota RTV 1140 CPX VHT four wheel drive, three cylinder diesel with power steering and a convertible hydraulic dump body allowing the unit to convert from a four seater to a two seater with an expandable bed. It is great for hauling equipment around the farm and for taking customers from their cars to the fields to rake. It gets a lot of use hauling brush, as well.

In 2012 I bought a 400 liter "Hardi" boom sprayer with PTO shaft from Lois Worcester. She and her husband had owned a blueberry farm in Kingsbury, and she was the Kingsbury town clerk for decades. In 2013 I bought another antique winnowing machine from Lois.

In 2013 we bought a 10-foot by 16-foot accessory building from Hill View Farms to house the future solar power system for the mobile home. Following the placement of the building, we bought a solar power system from Lee Goggin in Dover-Foxcroft. The system includes nine solar panels, and 16 six volt Rolls Batteries. The panels are attached to the south side of the building. It also includes a backup system that is hitched to the generator shed and a 6500 Watt Honda LP Generator. I used the Cat mini excavator to dig the trench 80 feet to the generator shed on the opposite end of the mobile home.

We bought blueberry fresh-pack processing equipment from Maine Blueberry Equipment in 2013, which included a feed conveyor, giant winnower, string table, slant table and ten foot pick-over conveyor. The system was discussed earlier in the barn set up chapter.

In 2022 we bought another flail mower. It is a five foot Sundown,

PHOTO: Solar Shed.

and it has a hydraulic slide feature that allows the mower to slide between rocks.

We decided to buy another Maine Blueberry Equipment walk-behind harvester that was in 'like new' condition from a Downeast Blueberry farmer. It serves as a backup for the one now in service.

PHOTO: *Mobile home solar panel set.*

It is amazing how much equipment one can accumulate during three plus decades. In addition to all of the above there were numerous used clearing saws, weed whackers, loppers, axes, hatchets, spades, shovels, brooms, ladders, air tools, hydraulic jacks, ramps, shelving for tools, bakers racks for blueberry orders, containers of all shapes and sizes for filling orders, tables and chairs, shelving for all kinds of new and used parts for maintaining the 20 plus internal combustion engines (down from the high of 32), flags and signs. The barn inventory fills a spreadsheet of more than 30 pages.

Chapter 18 — Rock Removal

We don't have rocks in the Midwest. But we saw them in calendar pictures. In Peoria County, Illinois, we had areas with 40 feet of loess and often a few feet of rich topsoil on top of that. But rocks? Landscapers would have them shipped in, and occasionally, in the more affluent developments, a site may have a giant rock on display near their entrance driveway. I often wondered how much they paid to have those shipped. What was considered a show piece in Illinois is a curse here on the farm. We have rocks! Rocks are just fine in the woods where they are not interfering with farming, but in the fields, No!

The early settlers of New England faced a daunting task of removing rocks from the land when they wanted to develop a garden or a place to build their home with a cellar. Frequently they would place the rocks along their property lines or the edges of defined areas such as a garden. The ultimate result was a beautiful stone fence or more commonly known as a rock wall. Those defined edges would vary in height and width depending upon how many acres needed clearing, and of course how many rocks were in the field. With winter's freeze/thaw action it causes more rocks to come to the surface, and some rock walls/fences grow in size over time due to the annual process of removing a new crop of rocks.

Perseverance Wild Blueberry Farm has some beautiful examples of rock endeavors. We have a few walls that are ten feet wide and up to four feet high. Kingsbury was settled in the 1830s, and the walls were presumably started about that time. With the wind and rain causing erosion from the ups and downs of the landscape creating soil build up around the rocks, I have often wondered how high would the wall truly be if I dug to the base of the wall?

It boggles my mind to think these rock walls were built without the modern hydraulic loaders we have on our tractors today. They were built one boulder and rock at a time with the use of a team of horses pulling a stone boat heavily loaded with varying shapes of granite to the edge of the field. The men would then place the rocks by hand on the earlier rocks thereby forming the walls that stand for centuries. As the ages pass many of the rocks are covered with lichens that try to break down the hard granite. Early stone boats were made of thick heavy planks forming a sled of sorts that was typically about three to four feet wide and roughly eight feet long, but the sizes could vary. The front of the sled (sometimes called sledges) would usually curve upward so it would not get hung up on the vegetation or uneven soil in the field. Chains were fastened to the sled to enable hitching the pulling team of horses. Some would have planks as runners along the bottom to reduce the friction while being pulled. The bigger the sled the more resistance and the heavier and harder it is to pull. Smaller is better. Ash was usually the preferred wood due to its durability. Later sleds or sledges were often made of steel which improved their ground friction because of the smooth steel bottoms. We have two stone boats at our farm; one is made of ash, and the other is made of steel. However, we do not have a team of horses. We use a modern tractor. It is a lot easier to care for a tractor than it is to feed and care for large animals.

For several years (mid-1990s to the mid-2000s) we used a cost share grant called EQIP, Environmental Quality Incentives Program, provided by the United State Department of Agriculture (USDA)

PHOTO: An example of the width of the rock wall near the Ames Homestead on the north end of the farm.

Natural Resources Conservation Service (NRCS) that provided financial and technical assistance to agricultural producers. The matching grant allowed us to improve the farm's efficiency by doing land leveling and rock removal. We did not do much land leveling, but removing the rocks allowed less damage to the equipment such as the tractors, harvesters and flail mowers. This resulted in less time working the fields because we do not have to maneuver around the rocks, thereby resulting in less equipment run time and more savings on fuel and maintenance.

We initially did the rock removal with a rock-bar, which is nothing more than an old truck axle with one end ground to a wedge shape. The length of the four foot bar gave us leverage to pry the rocks out of the ground. Frequently we would have to use two rock bars to manage a rock when prying it up. We also employed a chisel plow to loosen some of the rocks. The manual rock removal was not

PHOTO: Wooden stone boat.

as efficient as hiring a contractor but the limited amount of money available prohibited us from hiring a contractor.

In December 2008, I bought a 2002 Caterpillar 301.6 mini excavator. It has a hydraulic thumb which is great for being able to muckle onto the rocks to lift them out of the hole. The first day I used it, May 19, 2009, I threw a rubber track. I was flummoxed. I had no clue as to what to do to fix it. So I called the place where I bought it in Corrina, Maine. The gentleman was very helpful. He explained that I first needed to use the boom to raise the side of the machine where the track was loose and then remove an access panel on the track frame. There is a grease fitting inside that had to be removed and when doing so, a massive amount of grease came out. That released the pressure on the drive wheels and allowed the drive gear wheels to move inward on the frame so there was enough space to put the rubber track back on the drive wheel. After getting the track

PHOTO: Rocks, rocks, rocks and more rocks. South field, Sept. 2011.

PHOTO: Nancy and Let doing rock removal in Apple Tree Field Sept. 2005.

back in place, I put the grease fitting back in its threaded hole. As I filled the fitting with grease, the pressure pushed the drive wheel back, causing the track to tighten and stay in place. I was happy to have learned a valuable lesson that I have used many times over the years.

I have been told that mini excavators can lift more weight pound for pound than the big machines. I have been amazed at the size of

153

PHOTO: *Nellie prying out a rock with a four foot rock bar in the Apple Tree Field, Sept. 2005.*

some of the rocks I succeeded in lifting. I consider my little Cat excavator to be the best adult toy ever made.

It is important to stabilize the machine with the backfill blade on the front of the excavator. I put the blade down to the point that it helps put a bit if weight on it. On occasion, however, I have tipped the machine because I tried to lift and move a rock that was too big. That can scare the crap out of you. Usually, if I let go of the rock by releasing the thumb, the machine will right itself. Otherwise, I use the stick and boom to push the machine upright. I might add that it is extremely important to wear the seatbelt! Another technique I have used when tackling a rock bigger than I can pick up, is to dig a ramp from the hole and then drag the rock up to level ground and push it to the edge of the field with the backfill blade on the front of the machine. Sometimes I will leave it until the tractor is available and it can be loaded into the tractor bucket or pushed onto the stone boat and towed to the edge of the field. Beginning to dig rocks is like looking for icebergs. A rock may look small but, as I begin to dig around it, I may discover that it is almost as big as a car. I know there is no way I am going to pull it out of its hole. Another technique for dealing with this situation is to dig the hole bigger and deeper and hopefully push the rock into the deeper part of the hole. If I discover that I cannot budge it then it is time to admit that there is one rock that is going to stay put. Backfilling around it is the end result.

In July 2011, we hired Wynne Herrick's Construction Company to excavate a few of the huge boulders from the front field across from the former schoolhouse and move them to the rock wall along Preble Lane. They were already in the area removing a berm along Campbell Road. They were concerned about the mammoth size and

PHOTO: Lou with the mini Cat, June 2015.

PHOTO: Releasing the tension pressure on the excavator track by letting the grease out.

PHOTO: *One of the larger rocks pulled by the mini Cat, June 2015.*

weight of the rocks possibly cracking the boom on their big excavator.

The job was a huge success and that seven acre field is now pretty much rock free. There is one erratic that remains and will stay put because it has become a landmark on the farm. Of course, after the rocks are pulled from the earth there are holes. We order minus one gravel by the truck load in order to fill the holes which amounts to another arduous task, but it has to be done. Otherwise, I would get a tractor stuck when mowing or a deer, moose or a customer could step in the hole and break a leg.

Chapter 19 — Burning

For decades the standard practice for blueberry farming was to burn the fields after mowing. The Indians used to burn blueberry fields to control the weeds and improve the quality of the harvest. Burning had many beneficial outcomes. It reduces the slash from mowing and it releases the nutrients back into the soil more quickly.

Burning also helps control insect pests such as fruit flies. It also had some positive benefits in controlling fungus. It is not advisable to burn the fields if they are too dry or too wet. When it is too dry there is a risk of the fire burning too hot and burning the organic mat that is an important part of a good blueberry field. The mat helps to hold moisture and helps to stabilize the health of the field. Burning too hot can also damage the rhizomes of the plants and set back the production for several years. The organic mat is generally a few inches thick and is the result of decades of plant material buildup from mowing. If it is too wet you will not get a good burn and you waste a lot of fuel.

The downside of burning is the potential for the burn to get out of control. Some environmentalists complain about pollution and environmental impact. Wind is the ultimate enemy when burning, and despite no or low wind forecasts mother nature can throw a curve ball and suddenly whip up the strength of the gusts. To mitigate these concerns, it is important to have an adequate crew available with ample water usually in Indian tanks, and a standby water tank. A perimeter burn is done first before igniting the big burners.

When we first bought the farm, Let used his 100 gallon LP tanks on a setup behind the tractor. As he got older and the fact that the LP tanks were heavy, he replaced that system with a big red oil burner. The cost of fuel for the burners and the tractor adds significantly to the cost of farming. Add in the coins for the large crew to monitor the burn and stand ready with Indian tanks, and it can get costly.

About twenty years ago Nancy and the crew had the perfect morning to burn. Relatively no wind, not too wet and not too dry, and a full crew with Indian tanks at the ready. As the burn was underway the wind came up with strong gusts and the fire was temporarily out of control. The crew quickly stopped the spreading of the flames, but it was a scary reminder of how Mother Nature may change her mind. With that, new reports of controlled burning in other areas of the state getting out of control, and the increasing cost of fuel, Nancy declared that we were done burning. Not long after that I sold my fire trucks.

PHOTO: Barry and Jamie Catlin sitting on the landmark in the front field, July 2008.

PHOTO: Nancy's nephew, Barry using an Indian tank.

PHOTO: Let driving the tractor with LP gas burner.

PHOTO: Lou pulling an oil burner in a blueberry field.

161

In Closing

The farm has been good to us in so many respects. It has kept us active and introduced us to so many great people, including hard-working employees and long-standing customers. It allowed us to buy adult toys like tractors and harvesters, as well as a barn full of equipment. It has provided a learning experience like no other I expected in life.

There are several factors that are causing concern about the future of Perseverance Wild Blueberry Farm. As I noted earlier, our farm should not exist as a viable blueberry producer. We are very remote. We are not near any urban center, labor supply, or marketing outlet. The cost of equipment and maintenance has substantially increased over the past decade, and the cost of fuel has also more than doubled. We are more than 90 miles from the freezer plant in Hancock, ME. We are off the grid and rely on generators and solar panels for electricity to run much of the equipment. The climate has changed, whether you believe in climate change or not. The change has caused a significant impact on the blueberry industry. The cost of producing blueberries exceeds the freezer plants' willingness to pay.

To add to the above, we have also increased in age. The ability to work 15 to 16 hours a day and function on only five or six hours of sleep no longer works. Age has taken a toll on the body's output. Just as the equipment wears out, so do we.

When we bought the farm, we got bees for free, and the more bees, the more blueberries we got. We didn't get the honey, but we benefited tremendously from pollination. It wasn't long before we started to see a steady increase in the cost of renting bees. First, it was $25/hive, then the price increased by $25 increments over the next few decades until it reached $175/hive. The University of Maine Blueberry Cooperative Extension Service recommends two hives per acre. We run 50 acres per year, which would cost $17,500 for bees. We now rely on natural pollinators, but there are not enough to do as good a job as we would like.

The cost of labor jumped significantly when the state enacted annual increases to the minimum wage, which will exceed $15/hr. This now includes agricultural employees. The cost of fertilizer, herbicides, and insecticides tripled in one year, and that is if you can get them.

We have reduced the number of productive acres from 110 to less than 100.

I keep thinking this will be our last year, but my wife insists we might do it again next year. What will we do with the farm if we stop producing?

I do believe that the right individuals or families who follow us can make a go of it if they focus on value-added products featuring the sour-top blueberries.

We have been the caretakers of the land and not so much the owners. The land will be here for generations to come, as it has for many past generations. There could be an argument as to who owns whom. Do we own the land, or does it own us? If you do not take care of it, it will remind you of your responsibility. Ownership is a people concept that Mother Nature does not recognize. Our duty is to work with her and help her, help us. We need each other. It can be a great partnership.

Acknowledgements

Some say it takes a village, and some say it takes a team to put this narrative together. Others have said it takes guts. I would add that it takes perseverance.

It also takes the understanding of a great number of individuals who stuck with me during the enduring process of writing little bits and pieces for their review. They offered encouragement and constructive comments. For me, this started more than 35 years ago after I moved to Maine and started writing letters to my friends and relatives about the culture shock and the adventure of becoming a blueberry farmer. Those letters were the beginning of the writing exercise that carried on over the next several decades. I first began trying to write my autobiography, but as I retired and began spending more time with the farm and looking back over the tremendous experiences of building the business, as well as meeting so many wonderful people, I shifted gears. I believe it was late 2019 or early 2020 when I learned about the Piscataquis Writer's Alliance. My first meeting was at the Monson Library, and the members welcomed me. I felt I could get to like this group and as it turned out I still like them. They provide so much insight and encouragement that after this is printed I will again begin working on my autobiography.

My special thanks to all the past and present members of the Piscataquis Writers' Alliance which is now called the Piscataquis Writer's Group: Wendy Denney, Bill Macomber, Erik Stumpfel, Kevin

Trembley, Susan McCutcheon, Greg Wellington, Jo Eaton, Amelia Trader, John McNamara, Robert Meyer, and Kent Dellaire.

The many customers of the Perseverance Wild Blueberry Farm who have shared many stories and experiences and especially George Scott; Levi Cowett who shared personal history of the early years on the farm; our incredible staff: Robert Trottier, Lorry Polley, John White, and the many others that have come and gone over the past 38 years.

Most recently, John McNamara, who serves as editor and publisher of this effort. Amelia Trader who has served as the cover designer.

And last but not least is my wife, Nancy Buck Sidell, who tolerated my constant questioning as to who, what, when, where, and especially why.

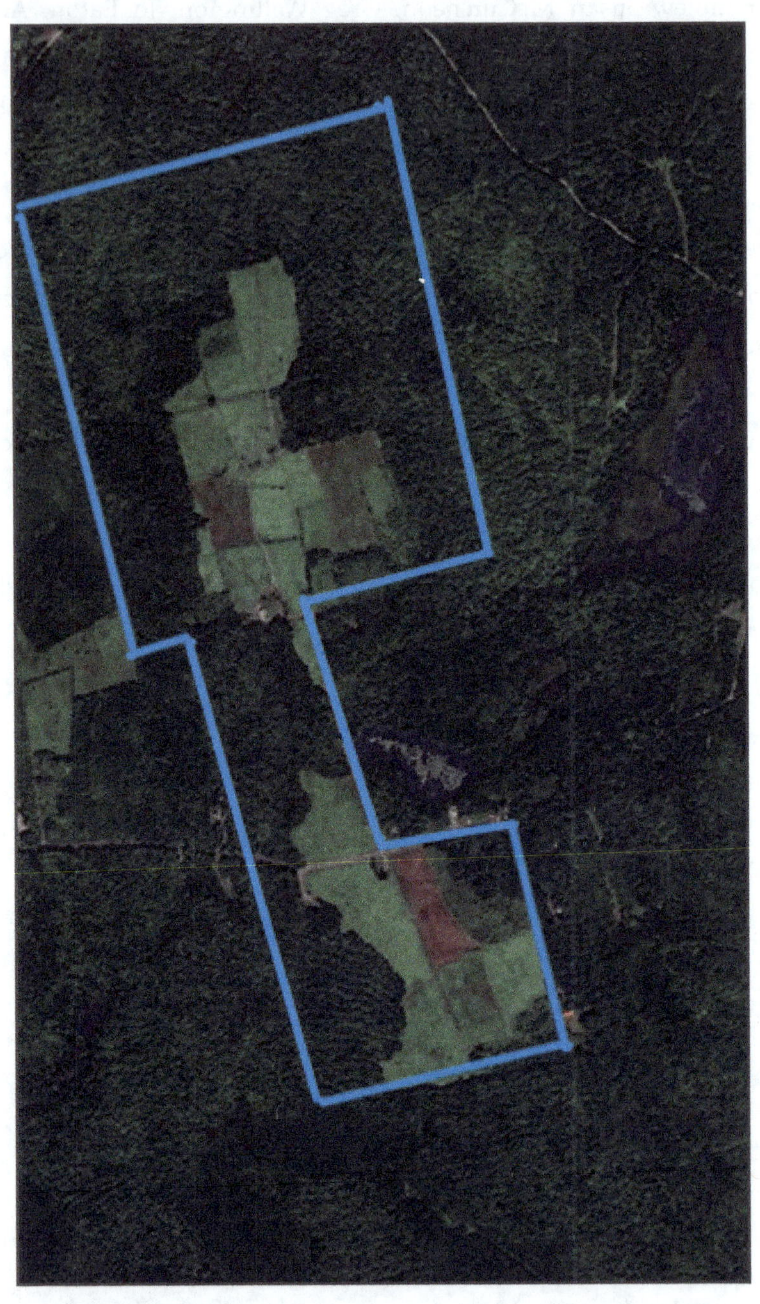

Approximate boundaries of Perseverance Wild Blueberry Farm, Kingsbury Plantation, ME. (45 degrees, 6' 58" N, 69 degrees, 36' 43"W).